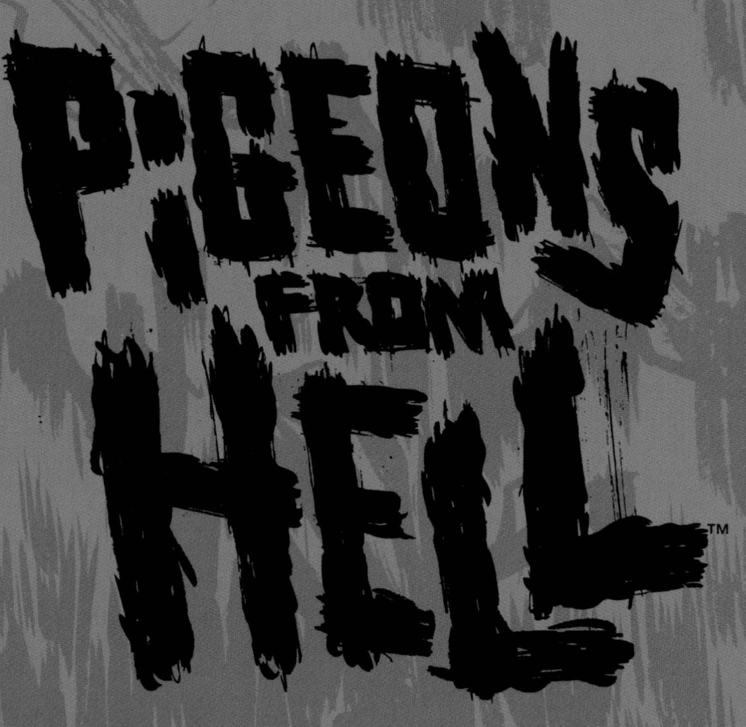

Based on the short story by
Conan creator Robert E. Howard.

WRITTEN BY
Joe R. Lansdale

ART BY
Nathan Fox

COLORS BY
Dave Stewart

LETTERS BY
Richard Starkings & Comicraft

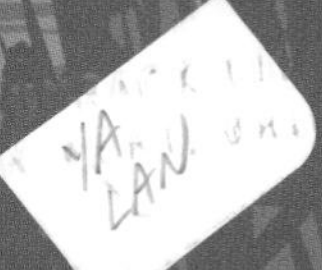

DARK HORSE BOOKS®

PUBLISHER
Mike Richardson

ART DIRECTOR
Lia Ribacchi

DESIGNER
Krystal Hennes

COLLECTION EDITOR
Philip R. Simon

SERIES EDITORS
Philip R. Simon
with Matt Dryer

ASSISTANT EDITORS
Ryan Jorgensen
and Patrick Thorpe

DIGITAL PRODUCTION
Dan Jackson

Special thanks to Jimmy Betancourt, Jim Keegan, Ruth Keegan, and José Villarrubia, and also to Fredrik Malmberg, Joakim Zetterberg, and Leslie Buhler at Robert E. Howard Properties.

Published by Dark Horse Books
A division of Dark Horse Comics, Inc.
10956 S.E. Main Street, Milwaukie, OR 97222

To find a comic shop in your area, call the
Comic Shop Locator Service toll-free at 1.888.266.4226

First edition: January 2009
ISBN 978-1-59582-237-6

10 9 8 7 6 5 4 3 2 1
Printed in China

This volume collects issues one through four of the Dark Horse comic-book series *Pigeons from Hell.*

darkhorse.com

ONCE UPON A TIME, THE LOUISIANA REGION KNOWN AS ACADIANA WAS HOME TO MANY MAGNIFICENT PLANTATIONS...

AND THEY ARE EMPTY...

WATCH FOR PIGEON POOP.
I'M WAY READY TO GO BACK TO AUSTIN. WAS GRANDMA PUNISHING US? THIS IS LIKE GIVING A DOG A TICK FOR A BIRTHDAY PRESENT.
CREEEK!!

SHE NEVER SAW THE PLACE, EITHER. IT'S AN INHERITED HANDOFF. THERE ARE STORIES THAT GO WITH IT. STUFF ABOUT VOODOO--OR *HOODOO,* AS GRANDMA CALLED IT.
NOT A GREAT ENDORSEMENT--BUT STILL, WE'RE *PROPERTY OWNERS.* IT COMES WITH ALMOST A HUNDRED ACRES.

I'LL TELL YOU WHAT SUCKS. MY PHONE DOESN'T WORK.
ALL YOUR FRIENDS ARE HERE, AT LEAST THOSE OF US WHO TOLERATE YOU, SO WHO YOU GONNA TALK TO?
YOU GOT A POINT.

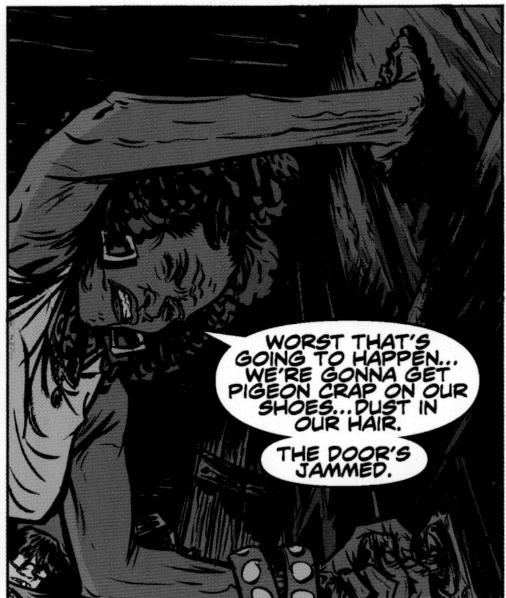
WORST THAT'S GOING TO HAPPEN... WE'RE GONNA GET PIGEON CRAP ON OUR SHOES...DUST IN OUR HAIR.
THE DOOR'S JAMMED.

KRIIK
KAUF
EEYUK!
KOF

"NOW THIS IS A TRIP."
"THIS NEEDS MORE THAN A DUST RAG AND SOME FURNITURE POLISH!"
CLAIRE. LOOK THERE.
COOO COOO
FWPP FLIP
COOO

JANET, DO YOU REMEMBER WHAT GRANDMA USED TO SAY ABOUT PIGEONS?
WAS IT... FOUR OF THEM AND A POTATO MAKE A GOOD LUNCH?

NO.
I DON'T REMEMBER HER SAYING ANYTHING ABOUT PIGEONS.
THEY'RE HARBINGERS OF DEATH. SHE ALWAYS SAID THAT.

"SHE WAS ALL ABOUT GHOST STORIES."
CHMM
CHMMM
I SAY WE LOOK AROUND-- SEE WHAT KIND OF PROPERTY YOU GIRLS HAVE INHERITED.
"WHAT I DON'T UNDERSTAND IS HOW GRANDMA ENDED UP OWNING IT IN THE FIRST PLACE."

YOU SHOULD HAVE LISTENED TO HER MORE. THE BLASSENVILLES LEFT IT TO ONE OF THEIR SLAVES FOR SOME REASON, AND IT GOT PASSED DOWN.
NONE OF OUR RELATIVES HAVE EVER BOTHERED TO COME HERE TO SEE THE PLACE.
YOU GOTTA SELL THIS DUMP.

YEAH, JUST THINK OF THE MEMORIES... PICKING COTTON... DOING LAUNDRY... DOCTORING FRESH WHIP MARKS--
HUSH!

IT'S SO HUGE.
WHAT I FIND CREEPY IS THAT WE HAD RELATIVES WHO WORKED HERE. AND IT WASN'T A JOB. THEY WERE SLAVES.

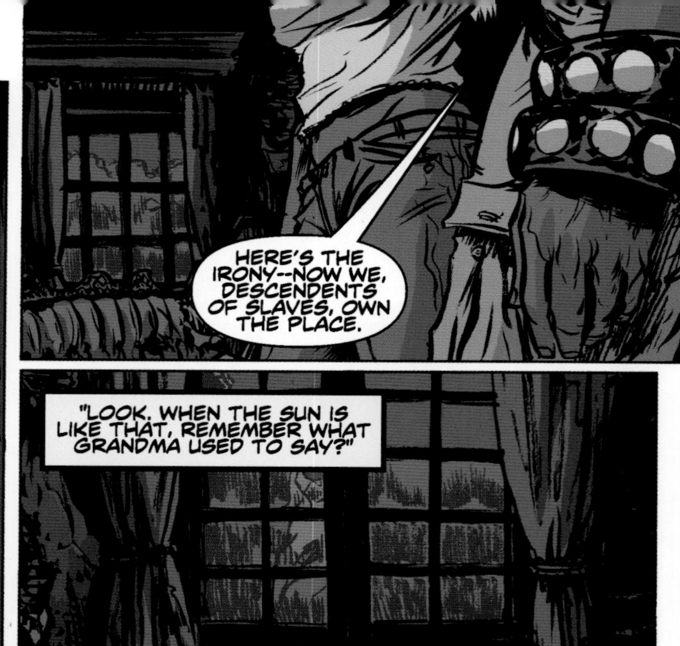
HERE'S THE IRONY--NOW WE, DESCENDENTS OF SLAVES, OWN THE PLACE.
"LOOK. WHEN THE SUN IS LIKE THAT, REMEMBER WHAT GRANDMA USED TO SAY?"
"YEAH. SHE SAID IT WAS THE GATES OF HELL OPENING... LETTING THINGS OUT."

YEAH. AND RIGHT NOW, STANDING HERE, I CAN BELIEVE THAT.
I THINK IT'S BEAUTIFUL.

LET'S ROUND THE GANG UP AND GET OUT OF HERE.
DO YOU SMELL THAT? LIKE SOMETHING DEAD'S IN THE WALLS?

HEY, FOLKS. YOU MIGHT WANNA SEE THIS.

THIS BETTER BE GOOD. THESE STAIRS DON'T LOOK SAFE. THEY'VE GOT ROTTEN SPOTS.

IT'S GOOD, ALL RIGHT. COME ON. HURRY!

HGK!

IT'S LIKE A PIGEON GRAVEYARD.

"ALL IN THIS ONE PLACE...? AND IT'S NOT JUST PIGEONS-- ALL THESE LITTLE CREATURES. DEAD."

NOTHING DEAD DOWN THERE. THEY'RE ALL PILED IN THIS ONE PLACE.
THAT'S BECAUSE THERE'S A HOLE ABOVE THIS SPOT AND THAT'S HOW THEY GET IN. END OF MYSTERY.
SO THEY ALL COME IN THE SAME HOLE, AND DIE IN THE SAME PLACE. WHAT'S WRONG WITH THEM MOVING AROUND, DYING SOMEWHERE ELSE?

ITS LIKE THEIR LITTLE HEARTS CAN'T STAND THE PLACE. THEY DON'T KNOW WHAT THEY'RE GETTING INTO UNTIL THEY COME INSIDE.
WHAT THE HELL ARE YOU TALKING ABOUT?
I DON'T KNOW. THIS PLACE ISN'T RIGHT. CAN'T YOU FEEL IT?

A BUNCH OF THEM HAVE GOT THEIR NOGGINS CHEWED OFF. I CHANGE MY MIND--THIS IS WEIRD.
CATS, MOST LIKELY.

I'M STARTING TO GET MAJORLY FREAKED OUT, CLAIRE. WE'VE SEEN THE PLACE, NOW LET'S GO HOME. BESIDES, IT'S COLD.
THAT'S ANOTHER THING. IT'S DEAD OF SUMMER, AND IT'S AS COLD AS A MEAT LOCKER IN HERE.

WHAT'S ODD IS--DOWNSTAIRS, NOT SO MUCH. IT'S LIKE THIS IS THE COLD SPOT. ONLY THIS FLOOR.

WAIT! DON'T BE SISSIES. WE'RE SUPPOSED TO BE HAVING A VACATION. THIS IS KINDA FUN, REALLY.
I'VE HAD ENOUGH OF THE TERMITE LOUNGE. I WANT TO GO.

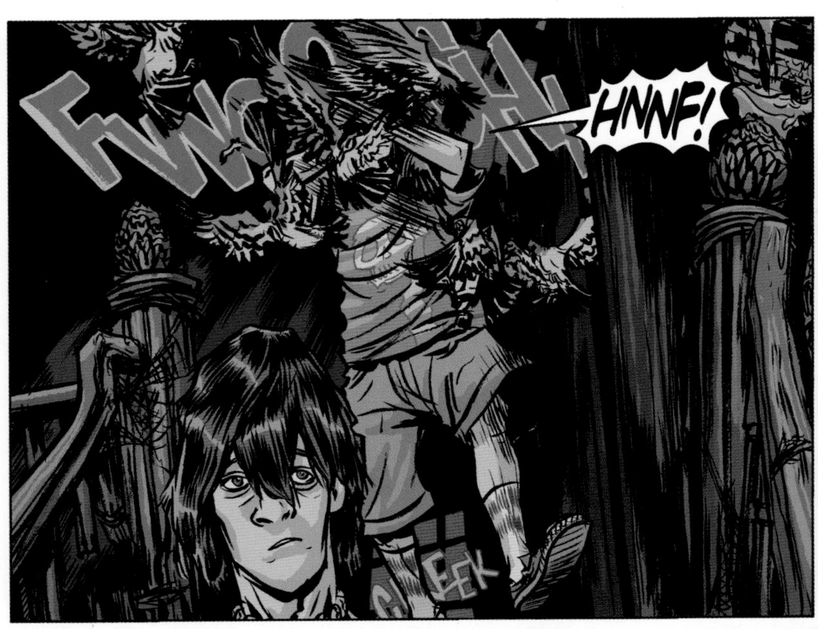
FWOOSH!
HNNF!
GLEEK

GYAAH!!

CRASH!

BILL! BILL! YOU ALL RIGHT?

DON'T LET HIM PASS OUT!
HE'S OKAY. CAN YOU TALK? HE'S OKAY.

I'M NOT OKAY! LEG...IT'S BROKEN. BAD. HRRG! IT HURTS. OH, GOD! I SEE THE BONE.

HE'S PASSING OUT! GOT TO GET HIM TO A DOCTOR.

HE'S OUT.
GOD! THE BLOOD!
PROBABLY BEST.

MAN. HE'S REALLY OUT... AND HE'S CLAMMY.

YOU'RE DRIVING TOO FAST.
I'M OKAY.

SKREEE

WATCH OUT!!
SHIIIT!!

TINK
TINK
BOING!

GET AWAY FROM THE CAR! IT GOES DOWN, IT'LL SUCK YOU UNDER!

I HATE WATER. I MEAN IT. I REALLY HATE WATER!
SALLY!

DON'T FIGHT ME, BILL! JUST BE STILL.

SALLY, COME ON! SWIM!

I DON'T KNOW HOW!

I'VE GOT IT.
WAIT!

LET HER GO.
SHE USED TO BE A LIFE-GUARD.

I GOT YOU.
I DON'T FEEL THE CAR ANYMORE!

OOOH, GAL, DO I OWE YOU BIG TIME.
YOU CAN PAINT MY NAILS UNTIL THE DAY YOU DIE.
DONE.

C'MON, SIS, YOU GOT IT!

HFF! HAH! I THOUGHT I WAS A GONER! I WAS WONDERING WHO'D END UP WITH ALL MY SHOES.
GOODWILL.

WHAT NOW?

GO BACK TO THE HOUSE, TRY TO MAKE BILL COMFORTABLE, THEN ONE OF US CAN WALK OUT.

OUT OF THIS SWAMP? AT NIGHT?! YOU'RE KIDDING! IT MUST BE FIFTEEN MILES OR MORE OUT OF HERE.

WE MAKE BILL COMFORTABLE, THEN MAYBE TOMORROW MORNING...

I'M FOR IT.
I'M IN.
I DON'T LIKE IT...BUT SURE...LIKE I HAVE A CHOICE.

I'LL GO WITH CLAIRE IN THE MORNING--OR SOMEONE ELSE CAN GO--BUT *TWO* OF US SHOULD WALK OUT. GIVE THE OTHER COMPANY. GET BILL A DOCTOR.
LOOK!

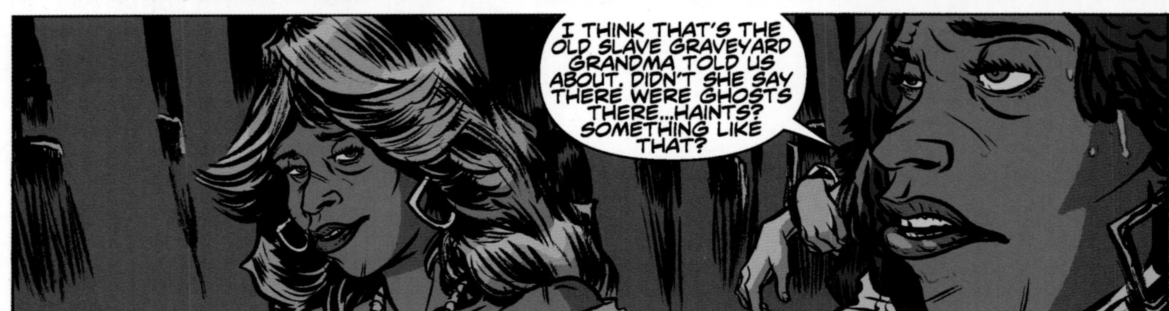

I THINK THAT'S THE OLD SLAVE GRAVEYARD GRANDMA TOLD US ABOUT. DIDN'T SHE SAY THERE WERE GHOSTS THERE...HAINTS? SOMETHING LIKE THAT?

"SHE SAID A LOT OF THINGS. SHE USED TO THINK THE TV REMOTE TURNED ON THE MICROWAVE, REMEMBER?"
"SHE WAS *SICK* THEN."
"NOW'S NOT THE TIME FOR GRANDMA'S STORIES. THAT HOUSE--AND WHAT'S HAPPENED TO BILL--HAVE ME KEYED UP ENOUGH."

I DIDN'T THINK I'D BE GLAD TO SEE THIS PLACE AGAIN.

YOU SEE THAT? SOMETHING MOVED IN FRONT OF THE WINDOW.

YOU PROBABLY SAW THOSE DAMN PIGEONS.
I DON'T THINK SO.
KRIK

LADIES, LADIES! I'LL CHECK IT OUT.
YOU'RE FREAKING ME OUT.
I TELL YOU, I DIDN'T IMAGINE IT.

NOTHING. I DON'T SEE ANYTHING.

"THAT DOESN'T MEAN I *DIDN'T* SEE ANYTHING!"

HE LOOKS REALLY BAD.
IT'S MY FAULT. YOU WERE RIGHT. I WAS DRIVING TOO FAST.
IT'S NO ONE'S FAULT, SIS. MAYBE THE DEER'S...?

IT'S REALLY COLD IN THERE NOW. *EVERYWHERE.* MAYBE WE CAN MAKE A FIRE AND GET BILL WARM. HE MIGHT FEEL BETTER.

I DON'T GET IT. IT'S THE DEAD OF *SUMMER*, AND I CAN SEE MY BREATH IN HERE.
WE COULD SLEEP ON THE PORCH.
CREEK
GRIK

I DON'T KNOW WHICH CREEPS ME *MOST*, SLEEPING ON THE PORCH OR IN THE HOUSE.
I'LL ANSWER THAT FOR YOU. OUT IN THE OPEN ON THE PORCH--THAT'S CREEPIER.

GET THE SUITCASES AFTER YOU DO THAT. WE'LL USE SOME OF OUR CLOTHES FOR BLANKETS.

THIS WILL MAKE A STARTER.
RIIP

WHERE'D YOU LEARN TO BUILD A FIRE? I FIGURED YOU FOR A *MICROWAVE GIRL*, ALL THE WAY.

GIRL SCOUTS. I LEARNED HOW TO MAKE A FIRE BEFORE I GOT THROWN OUT.

I'M SO HUNGRY I CAN SEE CORNBREAD WALKING ON THE GROUND.

SOON AS ITS LIGHT, I'LL GO.
AND I'LL GO WITH YOU.

THAT LOOKS LIKE IT'S GETTING INFECTED.
DAMN. HE'S REALLY BAD OFF.

HE'S STILL *CLAMMY*, BUT I THINK HE'S STARTING TO GET A BIT OF A FEVER.

I OUGHT TO GO TO SLEEP, BUT I'M TOO WORKED UP. TOO NERVOUS.
MAYBE YOU'RE RIGHT. I DID IMAGINE SOMETHING. OR IT WAS A PIGEON.

EXCEPT FOR PIGEONS AND VERMIN, I THINK WE'RE IT. BUT I'LL STILL BE GLAD TO GET OUTTA HERE.
HOW DID YOUR FAMILY COME TO OWN THIS PLACE, CLAIRE?

"WAY BACK, OUR FAMILY MEMBERS WERE SLAVES WHO WORKED ON THIS PLANTATION. AFTER THE WAR, THERE WAS NO ONE LEFT BUT ONE SERVANT WHO HAD BEEN A SLAVE.
"THE HOUSE WAS LEFT TO HER. IN THE BLASSENVILLE WILL.

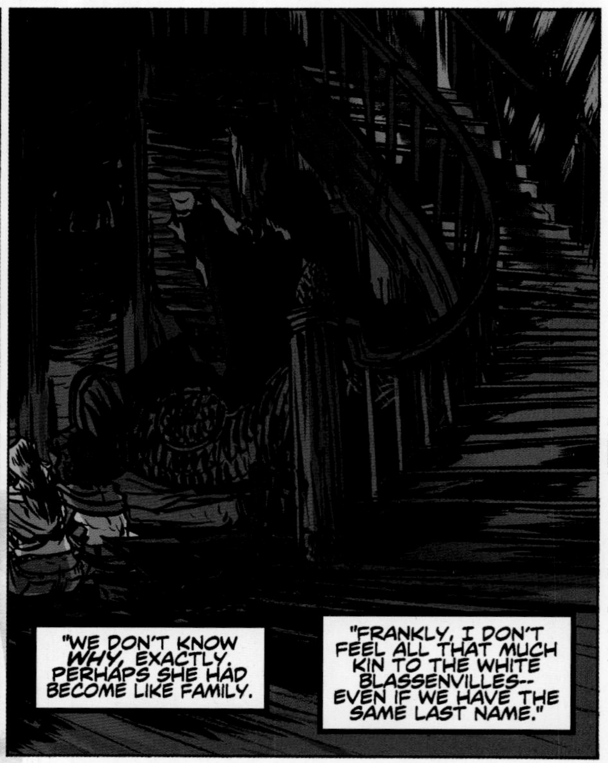
"WE DON'T KNOW WHY, EXACTLY. PERHAPS SHE HAD BECOME LIKE FAMILY.
"FRANKLY, I DON'T FEEL ALL THAT MUCH KIN TO THE WHITE BLASSENVILLES-- EVEN IF WE HAVE THE SAME LAST NAME."

FWUMP!

SHE WAS GIVEN THEIR LAST NAME. BLASSENVILLE. BEFORE THAT, SHE DIDN'T HAVE ANYTHING BUT A FIRST NAME. ANNABELLE.
IT'S BEEN PASSED DOWN FROM ONE RELATIVE TO ANOTHER, UNTIL IT CAME TO US.

WASN'T THERE A *CARETAKER*?
THAT'S WHAT I HEARD. THERE WAS SOME MONEY LEFT OVER, AND HE WAS SUPPOSED TO TAKE CARE OF THE PLACE FOR A STIPEND.
GUESS HE DOESN'T SHOW UP MUCH.

I'VE HAD ENOUGH OF STORY TIME. I'M GOING TO SLEEP.
IT'S AWFULLY EARLY.

WHAT ELSE IS THERE TO DO? BESIDES, CAN YOU BELIEVE THIS COLD?
THE WHOLE HOUSE IS *FREEZING* NOW. WE NEED TO TURN IN, START OUT FOR THE DOCTOR AT FIRST LIGHT.

I'M SCARED, CLAIRE.
IT'S ALL RIGHT.
YOU REALLY SAW SOMETHING?

PROBABLY MY IMAGINATION...GET SOME SLEEP.

MAYBE IT'S A NOISE. A FEELING.

AN ANCIENT SENSE OF SOMETHING DARK...ON THE EDGE OF REASON.

AN AWARENESS OF SOMEONE... OR SOMETHING... MOVING UPSTAIRS.

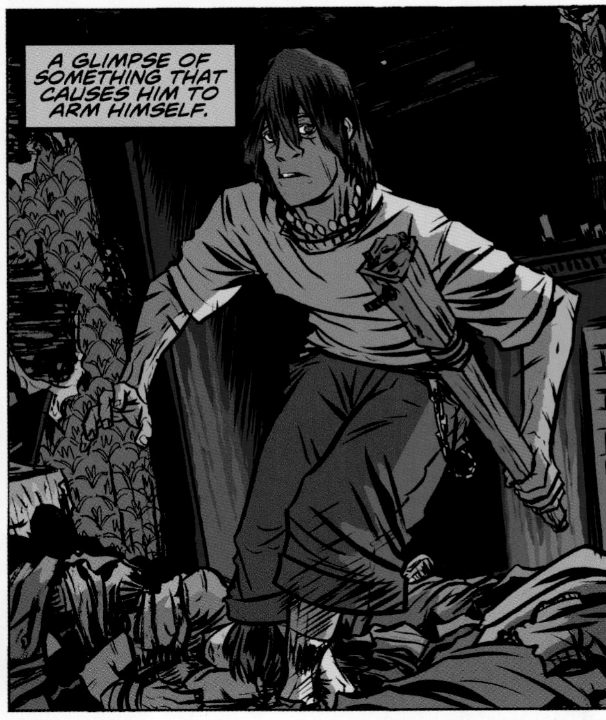
A GLIMPSE OF SOMETHING THAT CAUSES HIM TO ARM HIMSELF.

EASY, BABY!
DAMN, GIRL. I NEARLY BASHED YOUR HEAD IN.

WHAT IS IT? WHAT'S THE MATTER?
THOUGHT I SAW SOMETHING. HEARD SOMETHING AT THE TOP OF THE STAIRS.

PIGEONS?
I DON'T THINK SO. REMEMBER... CLAIRE SAID SHE SAW SOMETHING MOVING INSIDE THE HOUSE.
I THINK WE SHOULD JUST *LEAVE.*
CREEEEEK
RRT

NO CAR. MILES AND MILES AWAY FROM *ANYWHERE*. DEAD OF NIGHT. AND MAYBE THERE'S NOTHING HERE BUT MY IMAGINATION.
BUT I'M GOING TO CHECK...JUST LOOK AROUND A LITTLE.
SHOULD I WAKE THE OTHERS?

NO. STAY HERE.
NO PROBLEM.

THAT'S WEIRD. IT'S EVEN COLDER THAN BEFORE.

COME OUT, COME OUT, WHOEVER YOU ARE.

SUDDENLY... FEEL SICK.
MWWA-
THWAK

GET--

--BACK!!

JASON!

WHACK!
JASON?!

WAKE UP! WAKE UP!

SALLY...? WHAT THE HELL?

WHAT? WHAT IS IT?

THEM.

AT THE WINDOW. THERE WERE SHADOWS.
SHADOWS ARE EVERYWHERE, SALLY.
NOT LIKE THIS.
YOU'RE GETTING JUMPY. IT'S OKAY.
WHERE'S JASON?
HE HEARD SOMETHING. A NOISE. *UP THERE.*
HE WENT UP?
AND THEN I HEARD HIM *YELL*. THEN I SAW THE SHADOWS. THEY WERE LIKE PEOPLE, ONLY SHADOWS. I SWEAR!
THERE'S NOTHING OUT THERE.
MAYBE YOU DREAMED IT.
I DIDN'T DREAM IT. NOT EVEN A LITTLE BIT. I TELL YOU, THEY WERE THERE!

MAYBE WE SHOULD GO UP.
WHAT DID HE YELL?

I DON'T KNOW WHAT HE YELLED! IT WASN'T "FIRE" OR "COWABUNGA," IT WAS "EEEYA" OR "AHHH" OR I DON'T KNOW--
WHO GIVES A DAMN?! HE YELLED. IT WASN'T A HAPPY YELL!
EASY, SALLY.

CREEK
CREEK

MY GOD!
JASON!

JASON... OH, MY GOD.

CREEK

TAK

WHAM!

GET BACK! GET AWAY FROM ME!

WHERE'S SALLY?
DAMN! SHE'S STILL IN THE HOUSE. I THINK SHE RAN THE OTHER WAY.

YOU RISKED YOUR LIFE TO SAVE HER, AND SHE BOLTED.
I WOULD'VE DONE THE SAME THING.

"NO YOU WOULDN'T'VE--
OH, HELL. LOOK THERE."

THIS CAN'T BE HAPPENING.
JUST RUN, JANET! RUN!

WHAT... IN THE HELL?

CLIK
CLIP CLAK CLOP CLAT

WHAT IN THE WORLD ARE YOU GIRLS DOING HERE?

I DON'T THINK YOU'D BELIEVE ME IF I TOLD YOU.

TRY ME.
WE SAW... SOMETHING WEIRD.
AND OUR FRIEND TRIED TO KILL US WITH AN AXE. ONLY HE'S *DEAD.*

AND WHERE IS THIS MURDEROUS FRIEND?

THE BLASSENVILLE HOUSE.

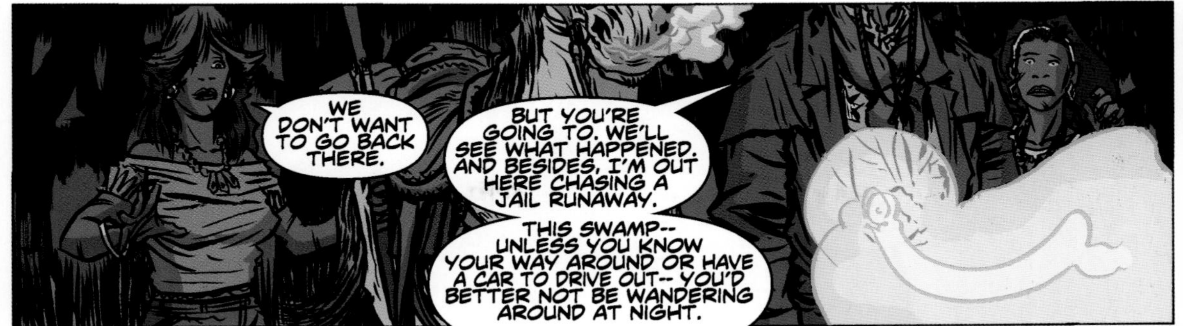
WE DON'T WANT TO GO BACK THERE.
BUT YOU'RE GOING TO. WE'LL SEE WHAT HAPPENED. AND BESIDES, I'M OUT HERE CHASING A JAIL RUNAWAY.
THIS SWAMP-- UNLESS YOU KNOW YOUR WAY AROUND OR HAVE A CAR TO DRIVE OUT-- YOU'D BETTER NOT BE WANDERING AROUND AT NIGHT.

THEN HOW COME YOU'RE ON HORSEBACK?
FOR OUT HERE, FOR CHASING SOMEONE THROUGH THE BOTTOMS, OLD GRANGER HERE IS BETTER THAN A CAR. MAN I'M CHASING, I DON'T THINK HE'S DANGEROUS...YOU NEVER KNOW...
...BUT I DOUBT I'LL SEE HIDE OR HAIR OF HIM AGAIN. TOO MUCH OF A HEAD START.

WE'RE TELLING YOU THE TRUTH.
WE'LL FIND OUT. IF SOMEONE HAS AN AXE, AND HE'S TRIED TO KILL YOU, THEN I NEED TO LOOK.

HE'S DEAD. HIS HEAD IS SPLIT WIDE OPEN. AND WE SAW SHADOWS THAT LOOKED LIKE PEOPLE.
THEY TURNED INTO A WOLF AND THEN SPLATTERED AGAINST CLAIRE'S BACK.

YOU GIRLS BEEN DRINKING?

MY GRANDMOTHER TOLD ME THE LEGEND. I DIDN'T BELIEVE IT. THE SHADOW WOLF. IT'S THE WILL OF THE DEAD. THEY DON'T HAVE ANY REAL POWER, THEY ONLY HAVE SYMBOLIC POWER.

I REMEMBER THAT STORY! I ALWAYS THOUGHT IT WAS JUST A TALL TALE.
I'VE HEARD IT TOO, AND IT IS A TALL TALE. YOU TWO THINK YOU'RE FUNNY.

DO WE LOOK AMUSED?
WHY ARE YOU GIRLS HERE?
MY SISTER AND I INHERITED THE HOUSE. ONE OF OUR FRIENDS HAD A BAD FALL.
NOW, SALLY, SHE'S MISSING... AND JASON...HE... HE GOT AN AXE IN THE HEAD.

AND HE'S THE ONE TRYING TO KILL YOU?
THAT'S ABOUT THE SIZE OF IT.

YOU DON'T MIND IF I QUESTION THAT STORY, DO YOU?
DO WE HAVE A CHOICE?
NO. YOU DON'T.

I REALLY CAN'T HANDLE GOING BACK IN THERE.
WE'RE GOING TO STICK TOGETHER UNTIL I GET TO THE BOTTOM OF THIS.
CREEK!

THUNK
THUNK

BLAM!
BLAM!

WHACK!

DEADER'N A TREE STUMP.

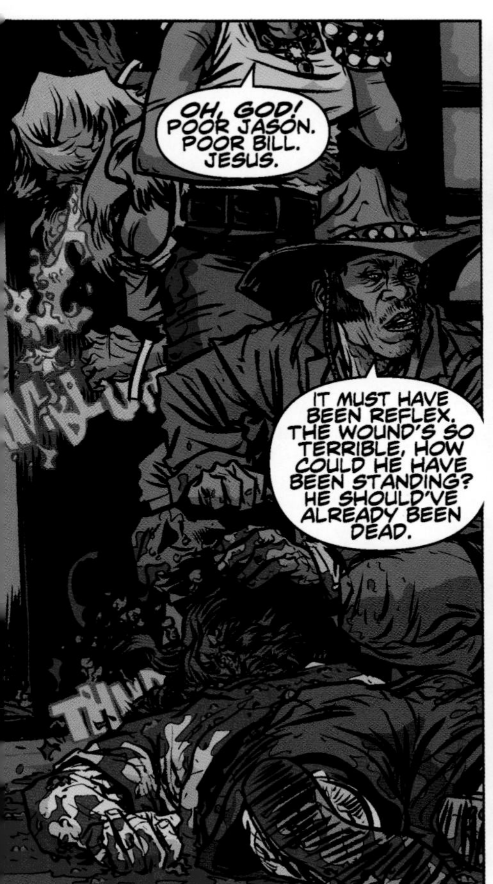
OH, GOD! POOR JASON. POOR BILL. JESUS.
IT MUST HAVE BEEN REFLEX. THE WOUND'S SO TERRIBLE, HOW COULD HE HAVE BEEN STANDING? HE SHOULD'VE ALREADY BEEN DEAD.

I DON'T KNOW THAT YOUR BULLETS DID IT. IT WAS MORE LIKE A PUPPETEER DROPPED THE STRINGS.
DON'T BE SILLY. WHO PUT THE AXE IN HIS HEAD IN THE FIRST PLACE?
YOU THINK IT MIGHT BE ONE OF US?

I DON'T TRUST ANYONE OR ANYTHING. BEING LIED TO IS A BIG PART OF MY BUSINESS. IT COULD BE MY JAIL RUNAWAY FOR ALL I KNOW.
HE COULD BE HIDING HERE, BUT IT'S NOT HIS STYLE.

STICK CLOSE. WE'LL HAVE A LOOK AROUND.
CAREFUL. THE STAIRS ARE ROTTEN. BILL FELL THROUGH... AND BROKE HIS LEG.
GRRT
REEK

JESUS, POOR BILL... HACKED TO DEATH...AND JASON. THAT AXE. THAT TERRIBLE AXE.

OOH. MY STOMACH'S STILL QUEASY.
WHAT A MESS.
I DON'T FEEL SO GOOD MYSELF.

I FEEL IT, TOO. IT'S THIS *PLACE.*
AND MAYBE SEEING ONE OF OUR FRIENDS WITH HIS BRAINS DRIPPING OUT CHOPPING UP ANOTHER FRIEND HAS SOMETHING TO DO WITH IT...?

OF COURSE. NOT TRYING TO BE INSENSITIVE, JUST FOCUSED. BUT...THIS HOUSE. THE AIR HERE'S SO...HEAVY AND COLD AND *FOUL.*
I'VE HEARD WILD STORIES ABOUT THIS PLACE. I DIDN'T BELIEVE ANY OF THEM, BUT RIGHT NOW, I'M NOT SO SURE.

WHAT ABOUT SALLY?
IF SHE'S HERE, WE'LL FIND HER.

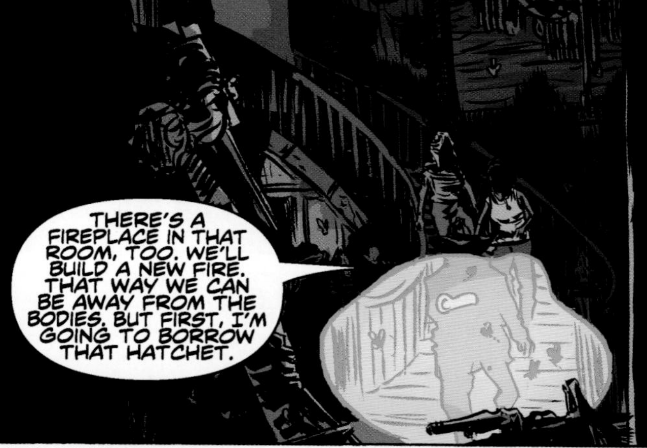
THERE'S A FIREPLACE IN THAT ROOM, TOO. WE'LL BUILD A NEW FIRE. THAT WAY WE CAN BE AWAY FROM THE BODIES. BUT FIRST, I'M GOING TO BORROW THAT HATCHET.

WAIT HERE... SOMETHING DOESN'T FEEL RIGHT.
WE WEREN'T GOING ANYWHERE.

DIDN'T I KICK THIS AWAY?
KRAK
KRKL
POK

A FEW MINUTES LATER...
SHOULDN'T BE COLD...BUT IT IS.
SHOULDN'T WE LEAVE?
I'M NOT LEAVING WITHOUT SALLY.

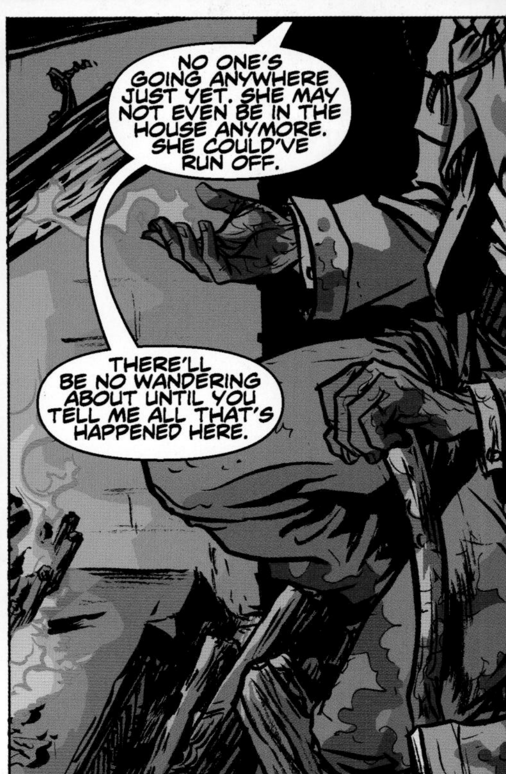
NO ONE'S GOING ANYWHERE JUST YET. SHE MAY NOT EVEN BE IN THE HOUSE ANYMORE. SHE COULD'VE RUN OFF.
THERE'LL BE NO WANDERING ABOUT UNTIL YOU TELL ME ALL THAT'S HAPPENED HERE.

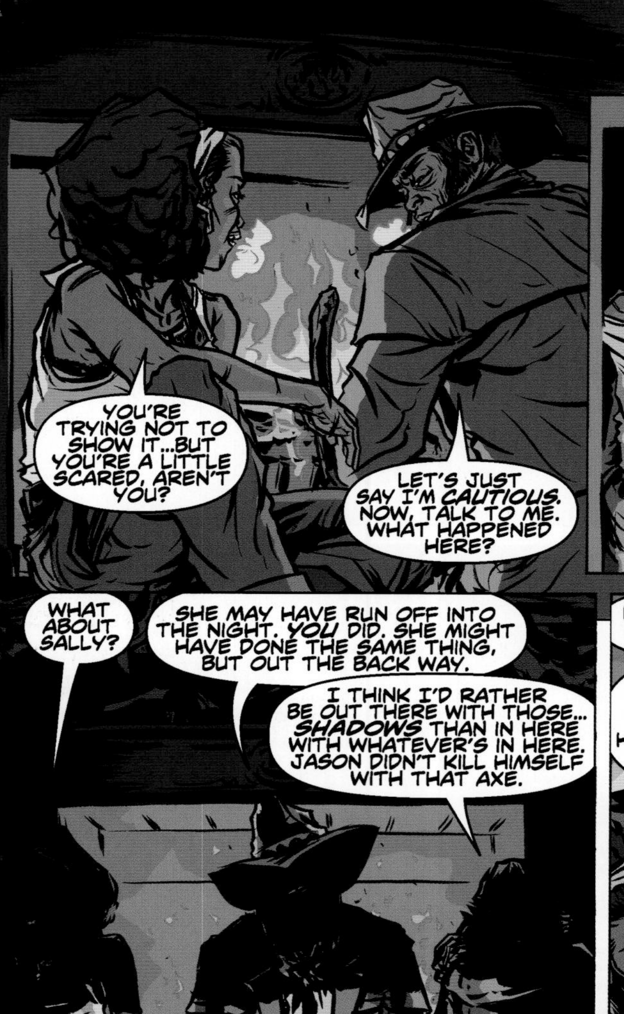
YOU'RE TRYING NOT TO SHOW IT...BUT YOU'RE A LITTLE SCARED, AREN'T YOU?
LET'S JUST SAY I'M CAUTIOUS. NOW, TALK TO ME. WHAT HAPPENED HERE?

...AND THAT'S IT, SIR. THAT'S WHAT HAPPENED.
NOT THE SANEST STORY I'VE EVER HEARD, BUT AFTER TONIGHT, I'M NOT SO SURE WHAT'S SANE AND WHAT ISN'T.
KSH- SHH
WHAT ABOUT SALLY?
SHE MAY HAVE RUN OFF INTO THE NIGHT. YOU DID. SHE MIGHT HAVE DONE THE SAME THING, BUT OUT THE BACK WAY.
I THINK I'D RATHER BE OUT THERE WITH THOSE... SHADOWS THAN IN HERE WITH WHATEVER'S IN HERE. JASON DIDN'T KILL HIMSELF WITH THAT AXE.
HORSE WILL ONLY CARRY TWO. AND THIS LATE, IT'S BEST TO WAIT UNTIL MORNING. SNAKES OUT THERE. ALLIGATORS.
WE'LL LOOK AROUND WHEN IT'S LIGHT. WANDERING THROUGH THIS OLD HOUSE AT NIGHT MIGHT NOT BE SUCH A GOOD IDEA.
YOU DON'T TRUST US. THAT'S IT, ISN'T IT?

BINGO... WHAT'S THAT?
SHFF
SHFF

I HEAR IT... SOMETHING'S COMING THIS WAY!
STAY COOL. I CAN SHOOT FASTER THAN A CAT CAN JUMP, AND I ONLY MISS IF I MEAN TO.

KLAK
SHFFT
SHFFT

DON'T HEAR IT NOW.

THERE IT IS AGAIN.

SHUFFFFT

SHFFT SHFFT

THAT DIDN'T STOP IT!

BLAM!

LET'S SEE HOW IT LIKES FIRE!

SORRY, JASON.

LADY, FORGIVE ME FOR DOUBTING YOU.

THEY SAY FIRE CLEANSES EVIL. I HOPE THEY'RE RIGHT.

WHAT'S THAT?

GUNS WON'T HURT IT.
NO. BUT THIS MAKES ME FEEL BETTER.

WE'RE GONNA GET OUT OF DODGE.

KRIK

KRAK

GGGRROWR!

HORSE GOT LOOSE!

JESUS!

AGAIN--
BULLETS WON'T
HURT THEM.
AGAIN--IT
MAKES ME
FEEL BETTER.

THEY CAN'T HURT US...THEY'RE JUST EMPTY SOULS.
DIDN'T DO MY BLOOD PRESSURE ANY GOOD.
MFF

"IT DIDN'T COME AFTER US."
"I DON'T THINK IT CAN LEAVE THE HOUSE."
"SALLY...WHAT ABOUT SALLY?"

WE'LL HAVE TO GO GET HER.

WHOA! NOT SO FAST.

I'M NOT LEAVING HER IN THERE WITH...THAT.
GOOD ENOUGH. BUT FIRST, LET'S REGROUP.

I THINK WE'RE AS REGROUPED AS WE GET.
MAYBE NOT. THERE'S ALCEBEE.

ALCEBEE?

HE'S OFF THE TRAIL HERE, AND HE MAY HAVE SOME ANSWERS. NO ONE'S EVER SEEN HIM OUT OF HIS YARD. MOSTLY HE STAYS IN HIS HOUSE.
WHY DO WE WANT TO SEE HIM?

BECAUSE THEY SAY HE'S A HUNDRED AND FIFTY YEARS OLD, GIVE OR TAKE TEN YEARS.
THAT'S *RIDICULOUS.*

IT'S WHAT THEY SAY. AND BEFORE TONIGHT, A LOT OF THINGS SEEMED RIDICULOUS. BUT IF HE *IS* THAT OLD...
...HE WAS AROUND WHEN THE WHITE BLASSENVILLES LIVED IN THE OLD HOUSE.

THEY'RE BACK.

THEY'RE HARMLESS, I TELL YOU.
THEY'RE STILL CREEPY.

LET 'EM FOLLOW IF THEY MUST.

I'VE ONLY BEEN HERE ONCE. AS A KID.

I DON'T SEE HOW THIS HELPS SALLY.

KNOWLEDGE.

QUIT YAMMERIN' THEN, AND COME INSIDE.
YES, SIR. I RECKON WE DO...UH, MEAN THE WORLD GOOD.

I KNEW YOU WAS COMING. I SEEN IT IN THE GUTS OF A CHICKEN.

GUTS OF A CHICKEN?
YOU CAN FIND THE FUTURE IN ENTRAILS, IF YOU KNOW HOW TO LOOK.
I'LL REMEMBER THAT. COME ON, GUYS, WE HAVE TO GET SALLY HELP.

YOU'RE RIGHT. THERE'S NO HELP HERE. I WAS GRASPING AT STRAWS. I SHOULD GO BACK AND FIND HER.
YOU TWO SHOULD WALK OUT. CHRIST. I RAN LIKE A CHILD.

SIT DOWN AND LISTEN.

NO PHONE OR CAR, IT'S BEST WE MOVE ON.
YOU'VE SEEN THE WALKING DEAD AND THE GREAT SHADOW? IT'S BEST YOU SIT.

HOW DO YOU KNOW THAT?
TOLD YOU. IT WAS IN THE GUTS.
TOOC
SLOT

I'M OLD, SO I HOPE YOU CAN STAND THE FIRE. MY BLOOD IS ALWAYS COLD, LIKE THE SNAKE.

THERE'S A GIRL IN THE OLD BLASSENVILLE HOUSE. SHE'S LOST IN THERE. WE SAW...SOME ODD THINGS. WHEN I WAS A KID, I WAS TOLD YOU WERE SOMEHOW CONNECTED TO THAT HOUSE, AND--
KSHH

I SHOULD HAVE BURNED IT DOWN LONG AGO...'CEPT I CAN'T LEAVE THE CIRCLE OF MY YARD. I'M TRAPPED HERE.

CIRCLE OF YOUR YARD?
I REDRAW IT EVERY DAY. AND EVERY DAY, IT TAKES ME A LITTLE LONGER TO GET IT DONE.
I GATHER MY SPELLS AND THE CHARCOAL FROM THE FIRE, THE ASH, AND I LAY OUT THE CIRCLE AND SAY THE SPELLS.

ONE DAY I'LL BE TOO OLD TO LAY OUT THE CIRCLE. AND THEN...I'M DONE. EVEN NOW, I CAN'T SEE GOOD ENOUGH TO KNOW I'VE DONE IT RIGHT.

IF YOU CAN'T LEAVE...HOW DO YOU EAT?
I RAISE A LITTLE GARDEN. I DRINK THE WATER FROM THE WELL IN MY BACKYARD. I EAT THE INSECTS THAT EAT THE WOOD OF MY HOUSE, SNAKES IN THE YARD.
AND THERE ARE THOSE WHO BRING ME FOOD. CHICKENS. FISH. WHATEVER THEY CAN SPARE.

YOU'VE ALWAYS LIVED LIKE THIS?
HEH HEH

IF YOU CALL IT LIVIN'. IT'S THAT *HOUSE* YOU BEEN IN THAT'S CURSED ME.

I AM THE *SENTINEL*. I WATCH. I WAIT.
I FIGHT.

NO OFFENSE, BUT YOU LOOK A LITTLE OLD TO DO MUCH FIGHTING.

NOT WITH THESE. WITH THE SPELLS OF MY ANCESTORS.

YA!
SPLAK
SPLAK
CRASH

YOU HAVE TO COME WITH US. YOU'RE EXACTLY WHO WE NEED.

NO. OUTSIDE THIS HOUSE, OUTSIDE THIS CIRCLE, I HAVE NO POWER. IF I'M OUTSIDE THE CIRCLE FOR LONG... I'LL DIE. THIS IS MY PATCH OF LAND. AND HERE I STAY.

MY BOTTLES CAPTURE THE BITS OF EVIL THAT THE THING IN THE HOUSE SENDS OUT. IT KEEPS THE THING WEAK, AT LEAST, SO IT HAS TO STAY WHERE IT IS.

BUT OUTSIDE MY CIRCLE OF POWER, MY HOME WITH ALL ITS CHARMS, I'M AS USELESS AS TITS ON A BOAR HOG.
THEN HOW DO WE FIGHT IT? WHAT ARE WE UP AGAINST? YOU CAN TELL US *THAT*, CAN'T YOU?
PLAT
PLAT

I WAS BORN IN THAT BLASSENVILLE HOUSE. I WAS BORN THERE SO LONG AGO THESE WOODS WEREN'T AROUND YET--JUST FIELDS FULL OF COTTON AND SLAVES.

THAT HOUSE... IT'S EVIL, AND IT'S MY OWN BLOOD MADE IT EVIL.

"ONCE THAT OL' HOUSE WAS THE CENTER OF A GREAT PLANTATION. BUILT ON THE BACKS OF BLACK FOLK.

"OLD MAN BLASSENVILLE WAS CRUEL JUST FOR THE SAKE OF CRUELTY.

"SO WERE HIS DAUGHTERS.

"MOTHER OF THAT DROWNED CHILD WAS MY GREAT-GRANDMOTHER, ANNA. SHE WAS A SLAVE AND A HOODOO WOMAN... AND SHE WAS A DAUGHTER OF MR. BLASSENVILLE.
"HE HAD HAD HIS WAY WITH ANNA'S MOTHER, MY GREAT-GREAT-GRANDMOTHER, WHEN SHE WAS LITTLE MORE THAN A CHILD.
"SHE KNEW THE OLD WAYS AND SHE CALLED ON THE *SHADOW IN THE CORN* FOR VENGEANCE.
"ANNA BROUGHT IT A BOWL OF HER OWN BLOOD MIXED WITH THE DIRT OF THE FIELDS. THE SHADOW HEARD HER PRAYERS.
"BUT THE DEAL HAD A PRICE... ALWAYS DOES.
"ONE MORNING, FOR NO REASON ANYONE COULD UNDERSTAND, OLD MAN BLASSENVILLE CUT HIS THROAT.
"RUMOR WAS HE HAD BEEN HAVING BAD DREAMS. COMPLAINED THERE WAS SOMETHING IN THE HOUSE... AND IT HAD COME FOR HIM.
"OTHERS SAW IT, BUT IT WASN'T AFTER THEM. YET.
"THING ANNA CALLED UPON IS A THING OF SHADOW. HE COMES, HE STAYS, DOES HIS WORK UNTIL HE GETS SENT HOME.
"NIGHT HE'S STRONGEST, BUT HE'S ALWAYS THERE, AND ALWAYS DANGEROUS.

"WASN'T NOBODY BUT ANNA COULD SEND THAT THING HOME 'FORE IT WAS DONE, AND SHE DIDN'T HAVE A MIND TO.
"MRS. BLASSENVILLE, LIKE HER HUSBAND, TOOK ANOTHER WAY OUT.
"STUFFED HER MOUTH WITH SALT BECAUSE SOME SAID SHE FEARED BECOMING A ZOMBIE. SHE'D BEEN AROUND LONG ENOUGH TO BELIEVE IN BAD JU-JU.
"SALT IN THE MOUTH STILLS A ZOMBIE... OR KEEPS A PERSON FROM BECOMING ONE.
"UNFORTUNATELY, THE DAUGHTERS REMOVED THE SALT. AND THE FATHER NEVER HAD ANY.
BRAK
SPLAK
"THE TWO BEAT THEIR WAY THROUGH THEIR COFFINS AND CLAWED UP OUT OF THE GROUND.
"DUG UP FRESH GRAVES AND SUCKED THE BONES. IF THERE WAS STILL FLESH ON THEM, THEY ATE IT.
"EVEN THE SLAVES THOUGHT ANNA HAD GONE TOO FAR. THEY CAUGHT UP WITH THE BLASSENVILLES ONE NIGHT, AND--

"--THEY WERE DISPOSED OF.

"THEN THE WAR WAS OVER, AND THE SOUTH HAD LOST.
"THE SLAVES WERE SET FREE AND THE DAUGHTERS STAYED...EXCEPT JULIA.

"JULIA WENT OFF WITH A YANKEE. THAT WAS QUITE A BLOW TO THE OTHER GIRLS.
"RUMOR WAS THE YANKEE, WHEN HE HAD HIS FILL OF JULIA, KILLED HER.

"BUT THAT THERE IS JUST A STORY. THE SHADOW IN THE CORN WASN'T GONNA LET HER GET FAR AWAY.
"SHE WAS DOOMED, LIKE ALL THEM BLASSENVILLES. AND THAT YANKEE, HE WAS IN THE WRONG PLACE AT THE WRONG TIME.

"IT WASN'T LONG AFTER THAT SARAH WAS FOUND UNDER THE PORCH WITH HER HEAD CHEWED OFF. WASN'T NO TERMITES DONE IT.

"THAT LEFT THE ONE STARTED IT ALL, DIEDRA.

"SHE MOSTLY JUST STAYED IN HER UPSTAIRS ROOM. AND SHE GREW OLD...QUICKLY.

"PLACE COVERED UP IN PIGEONS. ALWAYS A SIGN OF EVIL.
"THE HELP DIEDRA HIRED, SOME OF THEM FORMER SLAVES, SAID THAT THING WAS STILL IN THE HOUSE.
"IT WAS. AND IT WAS STILL ANGRY. IT SPILLED INNOCENT BLOOD SAME AS ANY OTHER.
"NOBODY WOULD STAY, NO MATTER HOW MUCH MISS DIEDRA PAID THEM.
"BUT MISS DIEDRA STAYED, AND THAT THING DIDN'T BOTHER HER. JUST LET HER AGE.
"THEN ONE DAY, SOME NOSY CHURCH PEOPLE COME TO CHECK ON HER. SHE WAS GONE.

"NO ONE FOUND HER BODY. NO ONE HEARD OF HER AGAIN. SHE WAS JUST GONE. AND THE HOUSE WAS THOUGHT TO BE EMPTY.
"BUT IT AIN'T EMPTY. THE SHADOW IN THE CORN IS THERE.
"THERE WERE TRESPASSERS, AND THE THING IN THE HOUSE DIDN'T LIKE THEM.
"OVER THE YEARS BAD THINGS HAPPENED, AND WORD GOT AROUND, AND PEOPLE QUIT COMING THERE.
"ALL THE SOULS OF THE BURIED SLAVES BEGAN TO COME OUT OF THEIR GRAVES.
"THE SOULS SOMETIMES TOOK THE SHAPE OF THEIR OLD SELVES.
"THEIR SOULS COULDN'T LEAVE, BECAUSE THE CURSE HADN'T ENDED. EVEN THE INNOCENT WERE BOUND TO EARTH UNTIL IT WAS OVER WITH.
"THEIR SOULS TRIED TO SHOW SIGNS OF POWER, BUT ALL THEY COULD DO WAS TAKE THE *SHAPE* OF SOMETHING POWERFUL.
"LIKE THE SHAPE OF THE WOLF. AND STILL... IT WAS NOTHING MORE THAN SHADOW.
"NOTHING OF SUBSTANCE.
"A HOPE OF POWER DENIED."

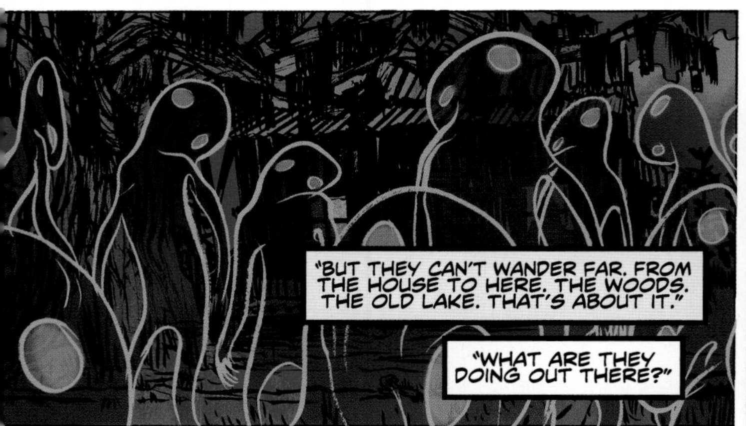

OVER THE YEARS, THROUGH MY SPELLS, AND MY POWDERS, AND MY PRAYERS, I HAVE LOOSENED THEIR SOULS FROM THE DIRT, BUT NOT FROM THEIR EARTHLY BONDS.

I HAVE GIVEN THEM *HOPE*, BUT NOT FREEDOM. THEY WAIT FOR THE DEATH OF THE SHADOW IN THE CORN. AND DIEDRA.

SHE STILL LIVES. FOR YOU SEE, SHE WAS ONLY A HALF SISTER TO THE BLASSENVILLE GIRLS. SHE WAS ALSO ANNA'S DAUGHTER. MR. BLASSENVILLE WAS THE FATHER.

"SHE WAS RAISED AS A BLASSENVILLE BECAUSE HER SKIN WAS LIGHT. BUT HER STEPMOTHER NEVER LOVED HER.

KRAK

"THE CURSE PASSED THROUGH ANNA, HER MOTHER, TO HER. ANNA'S BLOOD SAVED DIEDRA FROM DEATH--BUT IT DIDN'T SAVE HER FROM SOMETHING WORSE.

SHE WAS ALSO A BLASSENVILLE. SHE HAD TO BEAR THE CURSE AND KEEP IT ALIVE. AND SHE WAS JUST THE EVIL WITCH TO DO IT.
DIEDRA HAD MURDERED HER OWN BABY SISTER AND BROUGHT THE CURSE ON THE BLASSENVILLES, AND NOW SHE WAS THE CURSE.
BLUHK

NOBODY KNOWS FOR SURE HOW DIEDRA FOUND OUT WHO SHE REALLY WAS, BUT WHEN SHE DID, SHE TURNED EVEN MEANER.
ANNA CAME TO REGRET WHAT SHE HAD DONE. SHE USED WHAT POWERS SHE HAD TO MAKE THIS LITTLE PATCH OF LAND SAFE FROM THE HOODOO.

AND WHAT HAPPENED TO HER?
ALL MY FAMILY IS DEAD. THE HOUSE, IN ONE WAY OR ANOTHER, KILLED THEM ALL.

BUT YOU'RE SAFE HERE. WE'RE SAFE HERE.
MOSTLY SAFE. SOMEDAY SOMETHING WILL BREAK THE CIRCLE, AND DIEDRA--POSSESSED BY THE SHADOW IN THE CORN--WILL SEND A LITTLE BROTHER TO KILL ME.

A LITTLE BROTHER?
AN EVIL SPIRIT. IT CAN LOOK LIKE A SNAKE, A HAWK. NOTHING OF THE HOODOO CAN PASS WHEN THE CIRCLE IS FRESH, WHEN THE SPELL IS FIRM, BUT IF IT SHOULD WEAKEN... AND I'M NOT PREPARED...

"BUT THE COMMON WORLD CAN PASS. WIND, PEOPLE, ANIMALS. IT CAN BREAK THE CIRCLE.
SHF
SHF

"AND IF THE PROTECTION BREAKS, THE HOODOO CAN ALSO PASS.

"I'M LIVING ON BORROWED TIME."

YOU TWO ARE THE ONLY HOPE. BECAUSE YOU ARE BLASSENVILLES.
YOU ARE ALSO DESCENDENTS OF ONE OF ANNA'S CHILDREN'S CHILDREN... ONE SMART ENOUGH TO'VE RUN AWAY FROM HERE.

WE'RE SMART, TOO. WE WANT TO RUN AWAY.
NO. THERE'S SALLY.

WHAT EXACTLY ARE YOU PREVENTING HERE? OUTSIDE OF KEEPING THE SNAKE POPULATION DOWN.

I FEED THE SOULS THEIR SPELLS. LITTLE BOWLS OF BLESSED MILK AND SOIL. IT KEEPS THEM FROM FADING AWAY.
I KEEP THE SHADOW IN THE CORN FROM TAKING THEIR SOULS. IT'S ALREADY DUG UP AND EATEN THEIR BONES. BUT MY BOTTLE TREES STEAL SOME OF ITS SHADOW. SOME OF ITS POWER.

BUT YOU DON'T GO AFTER IT? YOU DON'T TRY AND DESTROY IT? YOU CATCH THE BAD STUFF WHEN IT COMES THIS WAY? AND ONLY *IF* IT COMES THIS WAY. WHAT KIND OF PROTECTOR IS THAT?

AN OLD AND FRIGHTENED ONE. MY MOTHER AND I TRIED TO DESTROY THE THING IN THE HOUSE. I LOST HER, AND I LOST THREE FINGERS TO THE SHADOW IN THE CORN.
I BARELY ESCAPED. SO I HOLD OUT HERE, WITH MY SPELLS, MY PROTECTIONS.
SO, YOU'VE FOUGHT THE WAR WITHOUT GOING BACK TO THE BATTLEFIELD?

I CAN TEACH YOU THE SPELLS. I CAN TEACH YOU TO TAKE MY PLACE WHEN I PASS.
I DON'T THINK I'D LIKE YOUR PLACE.
I CAN GUARANTEE THAT. BUT IT WOULD KEEP THE SHADOW IN ITS PLACE.

IT SHOULDN'T HAVE A PLACE. IT SHOULD BE DESTROYED. I'M GOING BACK AFTER SALLY.
THAT'S CRAZY.

THWAK
YOU DON'T UNDERSTAND WHAT YOU'RE UP AGAINST, LITTLE GIRL.

SHE'S RIGHT. WE HAVE TO GO BACK.

CRIIIIIIK
AGAIN, YOU DON'T KNOW WHAT YOU'RE FIGHTING. BUT IF YOU MUST--

DIEDRA IS STILL THERE, DEEP INSIDE THE SHADOW IN THE CORN. SHE IS A HATEFUL THING, MADE MORE HATEFUL BY THE SPIRIT.
STILL, SHE WILL NOT BE ABLE TO STAND TO LOOK AT HERSELF.
HOW DO YOU KNOW?

BECAUSE I'M THE MOJO MAN. I'VE SPENT MY LIFE LEARNING THE OLD WAYS. YOU...YOU KNOW NOTHING. TAKE THIS.

"SHOW HER HER FACE... AND FIND THE HEART."

THE HEART?
WHEN SHE BECAME THE SHADOW'S BITCH, SHE CUT OUT HER HEART AND HID IT. IT BEATS SOMEWHERE IN SECRET.
TAP
TAP

YOU CAN HOLD HER BACK WITH THE MIRROR. BRIEFLY. YOU CAN HURT HER AND THE THING THAT POSSESSES HER. BUT YOU CAN'T KILL HER UNTIL YOU KILL THE HEART.

THAT'S IT? THAT'S ALL YOU CAN DO?
LISTEN FOR THE HEART-BEAT...AND GOOD LUCK.

LISTEN FOR THE HEARTBEAT... AND GOOD LUCK.

DAMN.

I BROKE THE CIRCLE WHEN I DROPPED THIS STICK.

NO!

GOD, IT'S MY FAULT!
YOU DIDN'T KNOW...AND HE COULD HAVE JUST DIED. HE WAS SO VERY OLD.

BRRUB
BRRRUB
BRRRUM

SNAP

NO. IT WASN'T OLD AGE. IT WAS A LITTLE BROTHER.
QUESTION IS--WHAT DO WE DO WITH IT?

PUT IT IN WATER.

SPLASH

KLSHH!

PLOSH!

GIRL. YOU ARE ONE SMART COOKIE.
FOK

I WISH I HAD BEEN AS SMART. I BROKE THE CIRCLE.
NOT YOUR FAULT, KID. HE KNEW HIS DAYS WERE NUMBERED.
WHAT WE DO NOW IS, WE GO GET SALLY, AND WE TAKE CARE OF THIS SHADOW FROM THE CORN, OR WITH CORN, OR WHATEVER THE HELL IT IS.

YEAH, YOU'RE RIGHT...AND MAYBE THERE'S SOMETHING ELSE.

IF THIS KEEPS THE SPIRITS OUT, MAYBE IT WILL PROTECT US.
MAYBE?
MAYBE IS ALL WE GOT.

WE CAN USE STRING FROM THE TREE...TIE THEM AROUND OUR WAISTS.

IF SALLY'S DEAD, I'M GOING TO REALLY BE PISSED.
AND IF SHE ESCAPED THE HOUSE AND IS ON HER WAY INTO TOWN...? I SURVIVE THIS, I'LL KILL HER.

OUR FRIENDS ARE BACK.

I THINK THEY'RE WISHING US LUCK.

NOW THAT I'M HERE, I'M NOT SURE I CAN GO BACK IN THERE.
I'M *SURE* I DON'T WANT TO GO BACK.
I HAVE TO GO...

...FOR SALLY... FOR THE OLD MAN...FOR OUR FRIENDS.

YEAH, MAKE THAT TWO OF US.

THREE...ONE FOR ALL, AND ALL FOR SOMETHING OR ANOTHER.
WAIT A MINUTE.
KLAT

I CAN CUT A GROOVE INTO THE HEAD OF THE LEAD BULLETS, PUT A PINCH OF DIRT FROM THE CIRCLE IN IT, AND SQUEEZE THE LEAD SHUT AROUND IT.
WE DON'T KNOW IF IT'LL WORK IN ANY KIND OF WAY, BUT WHAT THE HELL?

PARDON ME IF I DON'T FEEL ALL THAT SECURE.
DON'T WORRY. WE HAVE BOTTLES OF ALCEBEE'S DIRT, AND I STILL HAVE THE MIRROR.

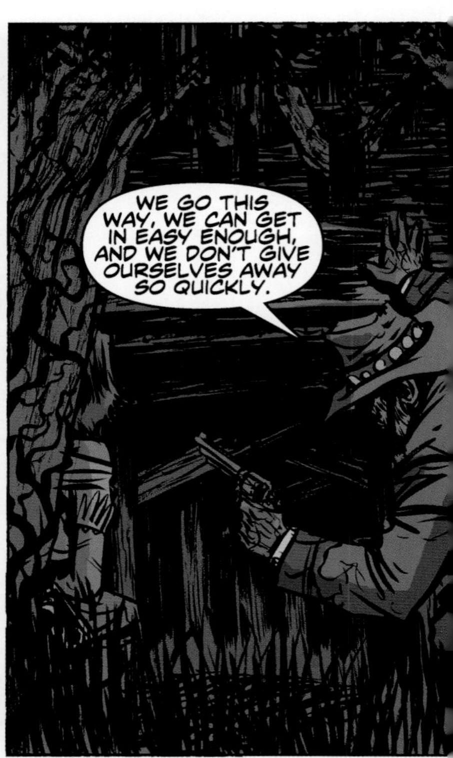
WE GO THIS WAY, WE CAN GET IN EASY ENOUGH, AND WE DON'T GIVE OURSELVES AWAY SO QUICKLY.

TNK
TING
SHFF
TA-TNK
SHFF
WE SHOULD STAY TOGETHER IS MY FIRST THOUGHT, BUT--
TNK
WE DON'T KNOW WHERE THE HEART IS.

IF WE SPLIT UP, WE CAN LOOK IN THREE DIFFERENT PLACES.
AND GET KILLED IN *THREE DIFFERENT WAYS*. DON'T YOU WATCH MOVIES? WE SHOULD STICK TOGETHER.
TNK

LET'S JUST HOPE IT'S TAKING A NAP.

IF ONE OF US FINDS THE HEART FIRST... DESTROY IT.
AND REMEMBER THE DIRT.
WELL, WE DO HAVE THAT. WE'RE FULL SCALE DIRTED UP.

I'LL TAKE UPSTAIRS.
I'LL GO RIGHT.
I'LL JUST GO SOME WAY THE TWO OF YOU AREN'T GOING. MAYBE OUTSIDE IN THE YARD.

FEEL SICK.

NO HEART. NO SALLY.
CLINK

GREEAAK-
RIIIK

DA-DOOM
DA-DOOM
GREEEAK

GREEEAK
BMMP

GRAK
SALLY!

AAAHH!

I THOUGHT YOU WERE...IT. OH, SALLY!

SORRY ABOUT YOUR FRIEND...BUT WE STILL HAVE TO FIND THAT HEART.
LET'S FIND CLAIRE. MY NERVES WON'T TAKE US BEING SPLIT UP. I DON'T CARE IF IT'S A GOOD IDEA OR NOT. I'M DONE.

PLINK

SALLY!

YOU SONOFABITCH! I'LL GET YOU!
I'LL GET YOUR ASS, YOU SORRY--

I'LL BEAT YOU TO DEATH!
OH, HELL!
I'LL KICK YOUR LUNGS OUT!
CLAIRE!
UHFF!

BE CAREFUL WHAT YOU WISH FOR, DUMBASS.
YOU MIGHT JUST GET IT...BUT NOW TO SEE--

--IF IT WORKS!

GREAT! I JUST PISSED IT OFF!

AND IT WAS MY BRILLIANT IDEA TO SPLIT UP.

CRASH!

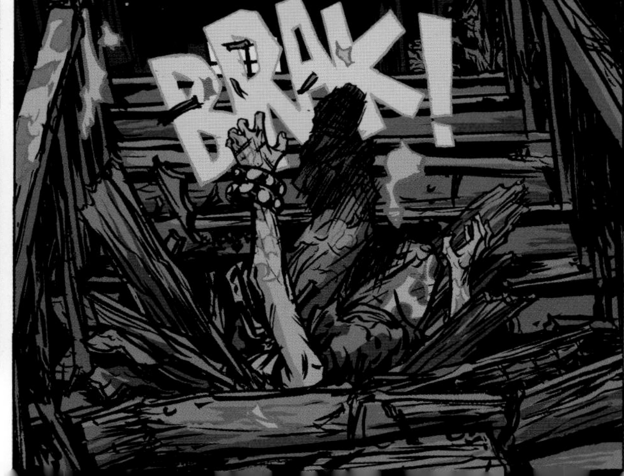

BRAK!

CRAK
OH, GOD! NOW I'M JUST STUCK HERE--
--WAITING LIKE A HOT LUNCH!
BRAK
PAK

BLAM!
THE BULLETS... THEY'RE WORKING!

BUT NOT WELL ENOUGH.

THAT'S IT! SPREAD THE DIRT OUT IN A CIRCLE!

SPLAK

MIRROR'S BROKEN--BUT IF THERE'S A BIG ENOUGH PIECE--

TAKE A LOOK, YOU BITCH!

THAT'S RIGHT! RUN!
SALLY'S DEAD, CLAIRE, AND WE CAN'T JUST SIT IN THIS CIRCLE FOREVER.
I KNOW. SO THERE'S NO USE STAYING. WE NEED TO RUN FOR IT NOW, COME BACK IN THE MORNING, FIND THE HEART.

I GET OUT OF HERE, I'M NOT COMING BACK. LET'S TRY THE KITCHEN... FIND A BACK DOOR OR CLIMB THROUGH A WINDOW.

WE SEE AN OPENING, WE BOLT FOR IT.

CREEK

SLAM

THE HEART...HIDDEN IN THE CANNED GOODS.
SMART HIDING PLACE. LIKE POE'S PURLOINED LETTER. IN PLAIN SIGHT.

SMART. BUT NOT SMART ENOUGH.

PLAT!

BLORTCH!

ARE WE ALIVE? DID WE GET IT?
PTANK

LOOK, CLAIRE. THE SHADOWS...THOSE SOULS...ARE FREE.
CREEEK

YEAH, WE GOT IT.
AND THE SHADOW IN THE CORN...THAT BITTER, CRAZY OLD BITCH... GONE.

THE THING WAS CALLED UP BEFORE, IT CAN BE CALLED UP AGAIN.

THEN LET'S NOT BE AROUND FOR THAT.
I FIGURE WE'RE GOING TO HAVE PLENTY OF EXPLAINING TO DO. AND MY GUESS IS...
...NO ONE'S GOING TO BELIEVE US.

RIGHT NOW, I JUST WANT TO ENJOY THE LIGHT...

...AND WE'LL CROSS THAT BLOOD-COVERED BRIDGE WHEN WE HAVE TO.
CRROOOC
COOO

NOTES FROM THE WRITER

When I was eighteen or nineteen years old, I discovered Robert E. Howard. I picked up a collection of his work, read the introduction. That introduction drew me to him and gave me a feeling of kinship. In the introduction, he talked about being a writer, how it was work of his choosing and he didn't have some son-of-a-bitch standing over him telling him what to do, and he had been able to make a living doing exactly what he wanted to do. Words to that effect.

In this respect I understood Howard, and since I had already, at my young age, had jobs with some son-of-a-bitch standing over me telling me what to do while I had plans to be a writer, this was an exciting statement.

I read all that I could find by him, which was very little in 1970, at least where I lived, and it wasn't until a few years later, after a divorce, some university time, and a lot of lousy jobs, that I became an active reader of Howard. Lancer was putting out the Conan stories, some of them modified or finished by L. Sprague de Camp and Lin Carter. I was living in Berkeley, California, then, and not far from where I lived, on Telegraph Street, there was a book and magazine shop with a lot of used books. I bought a batch of *Conan* books with the little money I had, cutting back on food and drink to have them, stacked them up, and read them when I wasn't looking for work. I found very little work, but I did manage to afford quite a few used Howard paperbacks. In time, I came back to Texas and began writing, and I kept reading Howard.

The stories that struck me the most, better even than *Conan*, were the horror stories, two in particular—"The Horror from the Mound," and "Pigeons from Hell." The latter hit me hard because I knew it from my childhood, in two ways. One specific way. I saw it on *Thriller*, a show that presented crime and horror stories every week, hosted by Boris Karloff, who had appeared in so many great horror movies I had grown up on. It may be hard to understand this now, but at the time, that "Pigeons from Hell" episode of *Thriller* was for many years the most terrifying thing ever shown on television. Later there were

others, but it was the king for many years. It was pure pulp, wood knots and all, and it scared the crap out of me.

The other way I knew about the pigeons was from my grandmother. She was Scotch-Irish, and she had told me about pigeons being harbingers of death; about how once, when a child was dying, a pigeon had appeared in the room, and when the child died, the pigeon flew out, taking the child's soul with it. This wasn't anything like the *Thriller* episode, but I remembered the bit about the pigeons and understood their significance in the TV version even more.

Anyway, years later, I'm reading Howard and I run across the story and have a flashback to my grandmother's tale, and of course the *Thriller* episode based on it. I almost let out a "whoop."

Over the years I've reread the story, and I've taught it in one of the creative writing classes I teach at Stephen F. Austin University. I taught it alongside Hemingway, and Fitzgerald, Faulkner, O'Conner, Twain, and so on. Howard's story is rougher in form, less sure in style, but in storytelling—WOW—it is hard to beat and connects students with the power of pure storytelling.

And so now we come to the comic. There was a faithful adaptation of the story a few years back, and I loved it. Anyway, it came up in a conversation I had with the folks who own rights to Howard's stories for film, and finally this conversation drifted to Dark Horse Comics. I have a minor history with Dark Horse, and I was anxious to work with them again. When the possibility of doing an updated version of "Pigeons" came up, I got on board.

I was reluctant at first. There's nothing wrong with the original story, or with the fine and faithful comic-book adaptation that was done before. But the thought was it might be nice to update it a bit, introduce new readers to the story, and perhaps lead them to the original tale and to all things Howard.

Updating was a bit bothersome at first, but I finally got in the spirit, keeping the center of Howard's story, the heartbeat of it, intact. In the end, I was very satisfied with the adaptation I did, though I hit a few bumps here and there and was wisely guided by suggestions from my editor. But the thing was, I was doing an adaptation of Howard's story, not Howard's story literally. Like it or not, I let Lansdale slip in. I was hired to do just that, and in no way would I suggest that Howard's story needs improving, but it's certainly fun to see an alternate version of his tale. If he were here now, I hope he would be pleased, and if not, I hope he would forgive me.

I like to think this is a fun adaptation, much enhanced by the beautiful and unique artwork that goes with it, courtesy of my collaborators Nathan Fox and Dave Stewart, and that it is an entertaining interpretation of my fellow Texan's work. I hope you agree, enjoy it within the spirit it was written, and understand that it is a love letter to one of my formative writers, the Great and Wonderful Robert E. Howard.

—Joe R. Lansdale,
February 2008

AFTERWORD
"The Brothers Gothic"

"It seems to me that the more wildly fantastic a tale is, the more likelihood there is for its being grounded in reality one way or another. The average human is so unimaginative that the highest flights of fantasy are beyond his power to create out of nothing." —*Robert E. Howard*

Robert E. Howard's friendship with H. P. Lovecraft was an inspirational and cantankerous thing. Their correspondence is legendary for their years-long debate over barbarism versus civilization (out of which sprang the seeds of *Conan the Cimmerian*), but there were other, equally important topics that sometimes get overlooked, such as their mutual fascination with folklore. Both Howard and Lovecraft sought out and collected regional folk tales and stories, as both were keen amateur historians with an interest in the history of their respective states.

In Howard's case, he had an embarrassment of riches from which to draw. He told Lovecraft in one of his letters:

"But no Negro ghost-story ever gave me the horrors as did the tales told by my grandmother. All the gloominess and dark mysticism of the Gaelic nature was hers, and there was no light and mirth in her. Her tales showed what a strange legion of folk-lore grew up in the Scotch-Irish settlements of the Southwest, where transplanted Celtic myths and fairy-tales met and mingled with a sub-stratum of slave legends. My grandmother was but one generation removed from south Ireland and she knew by heart all the tales and superstitions of the folks, black or white, about her."

Growing up in various towns during the oil booms of Texas, Howard was exposed to a number of "local" legends, tall tales, and ghost stories from well-meaning relatives and also the hired help. His storied relationship with "Aunt" Mary Bohannon, the former slave who told him folk stories and spun grim yarns about her cruel ex-mistress, helped supply one of the puzzle pieces that later became "Pigeons from Hell." In fact, it's possible to deftly reconstruct the plot of that legendary story by simply culling through Howard's discussion with Lovecraft over various ghost stories (Southern and otherwise) and regional folklore. This isn't a knock on Howard's prodigious imagination, either; it's one thing to transcribe an oral folk tale and quite another to stitch several folk tales together with a moving plot, compelling characters, and a gripping narrative pace. That's the genius of Robert E. Howard at work (or at play, if you prefer). Sometimes Howard was at his most effective when he was making a point about something.

Howard scholar Brian Leno penned one of the best essays in the past ten years of Howard studies, a persuasive piece called "Lovecraft's Southern Vacation." He convincingly showed that "Pigeons from Hell" was, in fact, the final word to Lovecraft regarding his dismissal of Howard's opinions regarding Southern folklore. Consider that the young protagonist of the story is a pale New Englander, usually paralyzed with fear, set firmly against the backdrop of Mary Bohannon's sepulchral house of horrors, and you'll see that Leno has a better handle on the tale than most of us. The secret, of course, was in Howard's usage of the gothic.

Dismiss from your mind the youth-culture-appropriated term; this is the real stuff. Webster's New Collegiate Dictionary defines gothic as: ". . . of or relating to a style of fiction characterized by the use of desolate or remote settings and macabre, mysterious, or violent incidents." Welcome to the swamps, folks. Zombies, hoodoo, crumbling plantation houses built on land that was old when the plantation owners got there . . . it's gothic in tone and gothic in scope, but with that Howardian twist—the flair for action, deftly told; sensory overload; and that amazing sense of urgency that forces you to keep reading, even when you don't really want to know what's going to happen next.

Over the years, "Pigeons from Hell" has survived the test of time. Most notably, it was adapted into one of the very best episodes of Boris Karloff's *Thriller* TV series in 1961. That television appearance may or may not have been the inspiration for the line from the Pretenders' hit single, "Back on the Chain Gang," but I don't know of any Robert E. Howard fan who didn't sit up

straight the first time they heard the lyric, *"Got in the house like a pigeon from hell."* In both cases, they are acting as harbingers of doom. Maybe Chrissie Hynde is a closet Robert E. Howard fan, after all. In 1988, the erstwhile Eclipse Comics printed, apropos of nothing, a painted graphic-novel adaptation of Howard's story, completely produced by Scott Hampton. It remains one of the most faithful adaptations of Howard's work, ever—not shying away from the material but rather embracing it—to produce a comic-book story that keeps the horror and sense of dread intact.

Of course, the story itself has been widely anthologized in over twenty Howard collections over the years. In the process, it's become one of Howard's better-known non-Conan stories, and is widely considered to be one of Howard's best stories, period. "Pigeons from Hell" continues to thrill and chill despite the now-quaint-sounding title because those Gothic themes that Howard tapped into never really went away. The old houses, the swamps, the sense of age . . . it's all still out there, and you only need drive through one good "dead zone" late at night, where there's no cell-phone activity, no street lights, no nothing except rows of trees and two lanes of blacktop, to really start feeling that sense of dread . . . no, those old stories never really die. And no one knows that better than Joe Lansdale.

"At night, when I closed my eyes, I saw Mose hanging, his pants down, cut, bleeding, his eyes and tongue bulged, that rope around his neck. It would be some time before I could lay down and not have that image jump immediately to mind, and some years before it didn't come back to me on a regular basis. Funny things would set it off. Just seeing a rope, or a certain kind of limb on an oak, or even the way sunlight might be falling through limbs and leaves.

"Even now, from time to time, it comes back to me clear, as if it happened day before yesterday."

—Joe Lansdale, from The Bottoms

For a long time now, I've considered Joe Lansdale as the heir to Howard's legacy as the Edgar Allan Poe of Texas. This is not to say that Joe writes like Robert E. Howard. He doesn't. He writes like Joe Lansdale, much in the same way that Robert E. Howard always wrote like Robert E. Howard. Joe's fiction is both genre bending and genre busting, and no matter what he's writing, his prose is always leavened with equal parts vivid action and vibrant description. He's not afraid, either, to write exactly what he wants to write and tell the stories he wants to tell, with no compromises or apologies. Moreover, Joe's voice—that tone and turn of phrase which is critical to an author's storytelling ability—is unique. You just know when you're reading a Joe Lansdale story; you usually feel it in your guts.

Joe is a vocal admirer of Robert E. Howard, and credits the Texas author with helping to point the way in his own enviable career. Joe has often remarked on the similarities between the two of them: growing up in a rural and

somewhat uneducated environment that emphasized physical culture over book smarts; the shared interests in boxing and martial arts; the sense of small-town isolation that comes from being the only reader or writer in your vicinity; and that self-guided mentality of reading and enjoying a variety of different stories, from comics and pulps to movies and literature. All of that stimuli went in at equal value; no one dictated their tastes and told them what was high art and what was trash.

Growing up in East Texas, Joe also got a hefty dose of oral folk tales, ghost stories, and no small amount of tall lying from the various bullshitters in his life (in Texas, that's an affectionate term). Joe himself spins a hell of a yarn, both in person and in print. Joe also grew up in the wilderness of the Piney Woods (not unlike the setting in his Edgar Award–winning novel, *The Bottoms*), and so like Howard summoning up his memories of Bagwell, Texas, and Louisiana in his writing of "Pigeons from Hell," Joe was able to scare the bejeezus out of himself the first time he read the story because, by and large, he was living in it.

Sometimes we think about the one or two dead and/or famous people we'd like to meet, with the usual set of party-driven answers. But if I had my way, I'd get Robert E. Howard and Joe R. Lansdale in a room together, ask them who they think is a bigger liar, and then just sit back and listen as they worked their magic, trying to out-story one another. It makes me chuckle just to think about it. Lying isn't the only skill a good writer needs, but in Texas, where we literally grow up steeped in the state's mythology, it's a necessity for survival.

Maybe it's fitting that, years later, with over two hundred short stories and twoscore novels under his belt, and in the position to be able to write pretty much whatever he damn well feels like writing, Joe would be asked by Dark Horse to come play in Robert E. Howard's sandbox. In many ways, Joe is the perfect fit to adapt and work with Howard's stories and concepts because he's both respectful of the material and he's not afraid to bring his own sensibilities to whatever he's working on. If you want to read Howard, then go read Howard, in other words. When you are tasked with the job of updating "Pigeons from Hell," how on Earth do you walk that fine line between respect and relevance?

Don't ask me how, but Joe did it. By keeping all of the major set pieces and action sequences, but updating the story into the twenty-first century, he was able to frame the tale as a sequel and still have it be suspenseful and creepy to readers who already know how it's going to play out. Of particular interest is the fact that Joe got to do what not even Howard was able to do, and that's provide an ending to the story. But what really helped to sell the whole package was the overall gothic tone. The spirits in the swamp, the pigeons on the veranda, the thing at the top of the stairs . . . it all had a sense of inevitable doom about it in that we were repeating the history of Blassenville Manor yet again as readers. Thanks to

Joe's ending, we are finally allowed to see the house merely as a house, finally at peace, and the past at last allowed to dim and fade away.

These kinds of projects are twofold: first off, they are great entertainment, utilizing the material of an author who doesn't always get a fair shake by people who profess to admire him. Second, they pique the interest of fans who want to know more and read more about this bright young man who created so much, so intensely, and then left us so quickly. Whether Dark Horse is updating the Robert E. Howard canon for a new audience or adapting his stories directly to present them in a new and different way, it's the spirit of Robert E. Howard that shines through these projects when they are at their very best.

Thanks are due, then, to Joe and Nathan and Dave for taking the ball and running with it, for setting the bar for other adaptations to come, and for making it all look so easy. To the readers as well, who blogged their interest and kept the support high, and to the fans who are not only being supportive but also encouraging, thanks very much. Now, go read some Robert E. Howard, will you?

Mark Finn
Somewhere in North Texas
August 25, 2008

PIGEONS FROM HELL
Cover Gallery

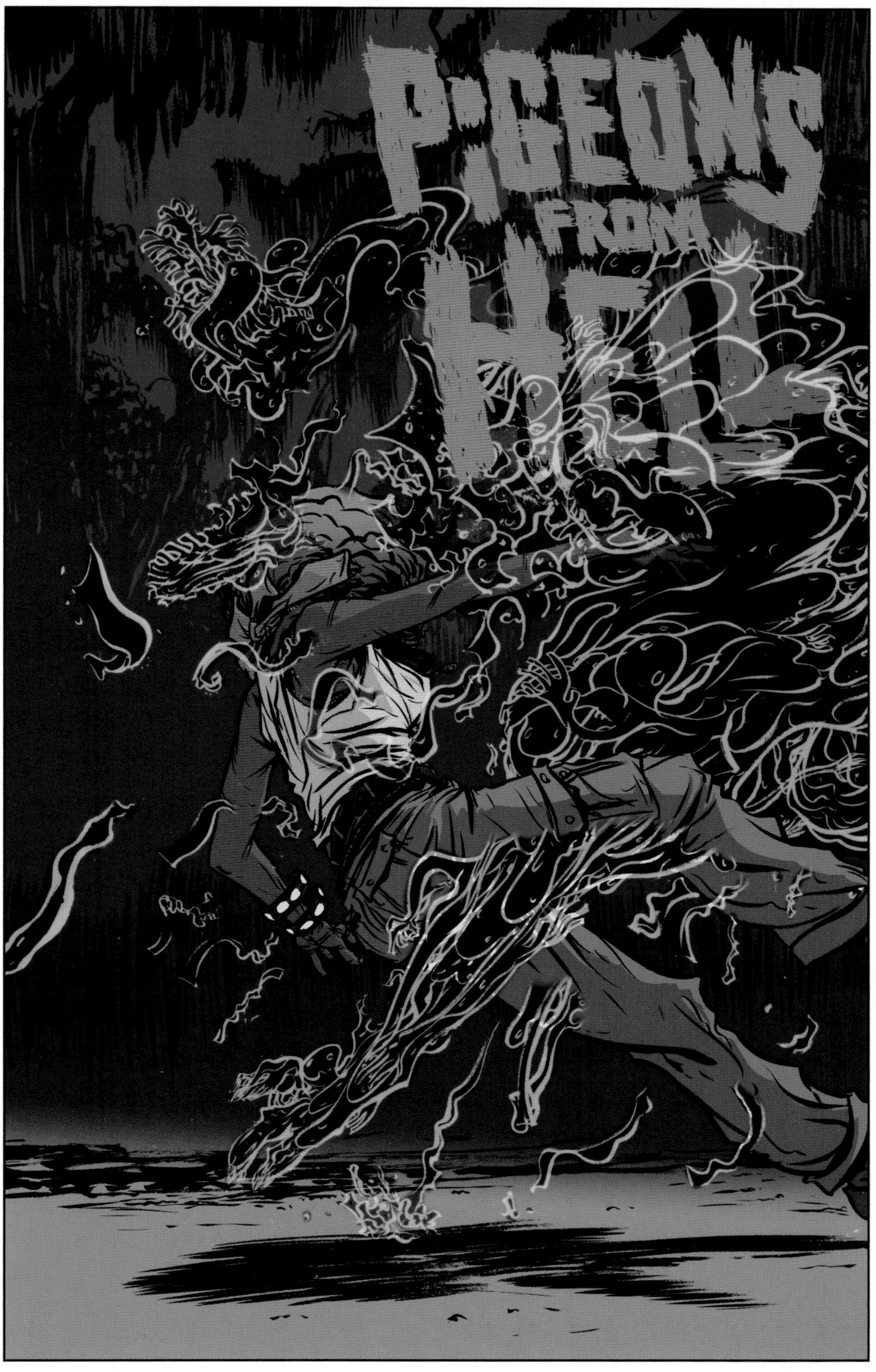

Front cover of this collection: a modified version of the cover for *Pigeons from Hell* #1, with art by Nathan Fox and colors by Dave Stewart. This page: *Pigeons from Hell* #2—cover art and colors by Nathan Fox.

Pigeons from Hell #3 cover art by Nathan Fox, with colors by José Villarrubia.

Pigeons from Hell #4 cover art and colors by Nathan Fox.

THE SKETCHBOOK FROM HELL

with commentary from artist Nathan Fox

When we first started designing the characters, I really wanted to make the shadow creatures and their shadow wolf as unique as I could—otherworldly, if possible. They weren't quite ghosts or traditional specters. They were described as flat, inky, and transparent, and they were the souls of those killed by the shadow in the corn creature. Simple forms seemed the most appropriate for some reason, so that's how they ended up—as playful, but creepy, glowing-eyed shadows.

The shadow wolf is constructed out of all the shadow creatures swirling together and transforming as a group into the wolf. Their hands, arms, and fingers layer together to make the jaws and teeth, their arms and legs form a bushy tail, and so on . . . For the final pages, all of the wolf and shadow creatures' images were drawn onto a separate layer of vellum from the final inks so that Dave could do his magic with them colorwise, and they would appear to float on top of all the line work and characters.

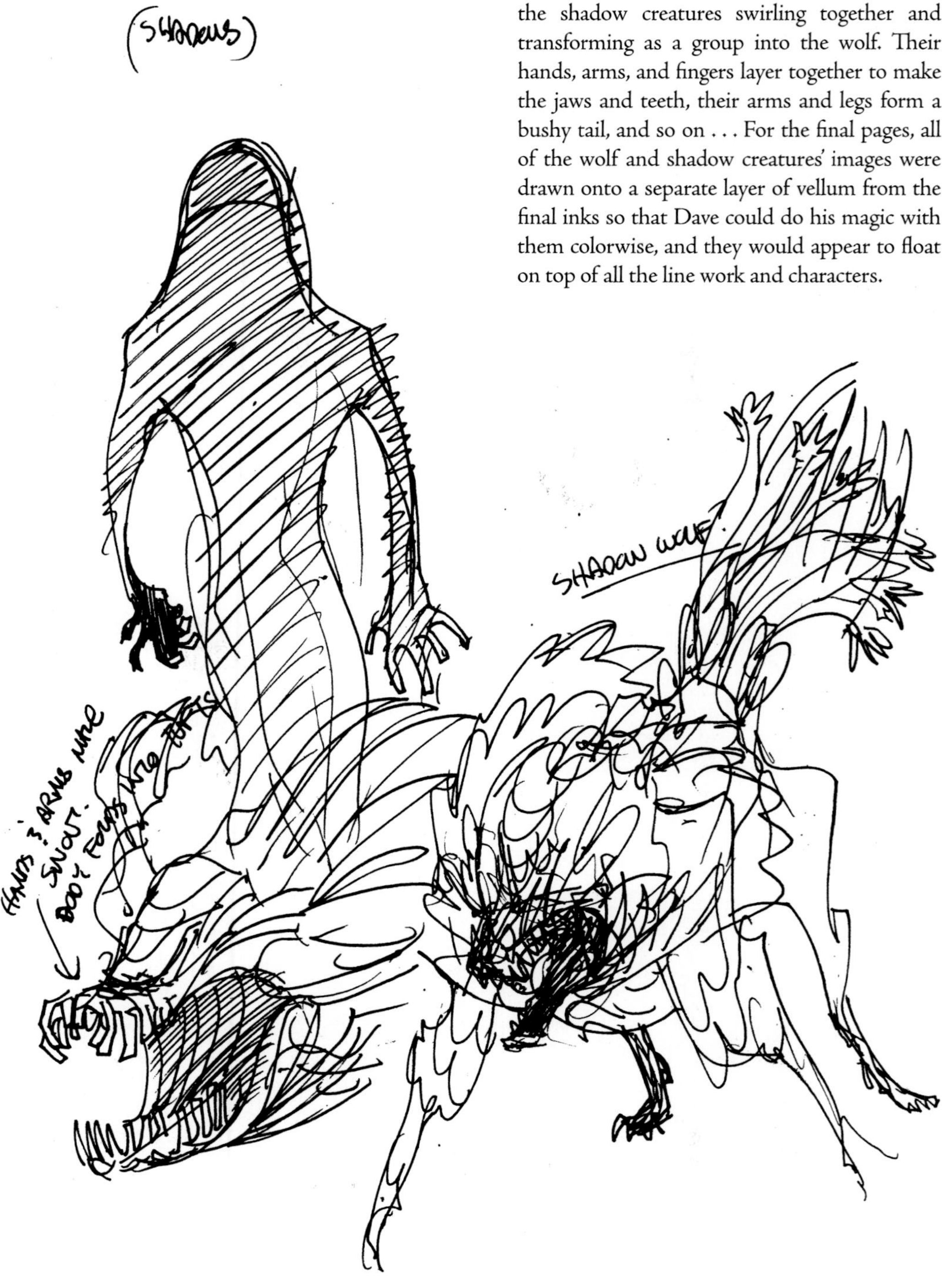

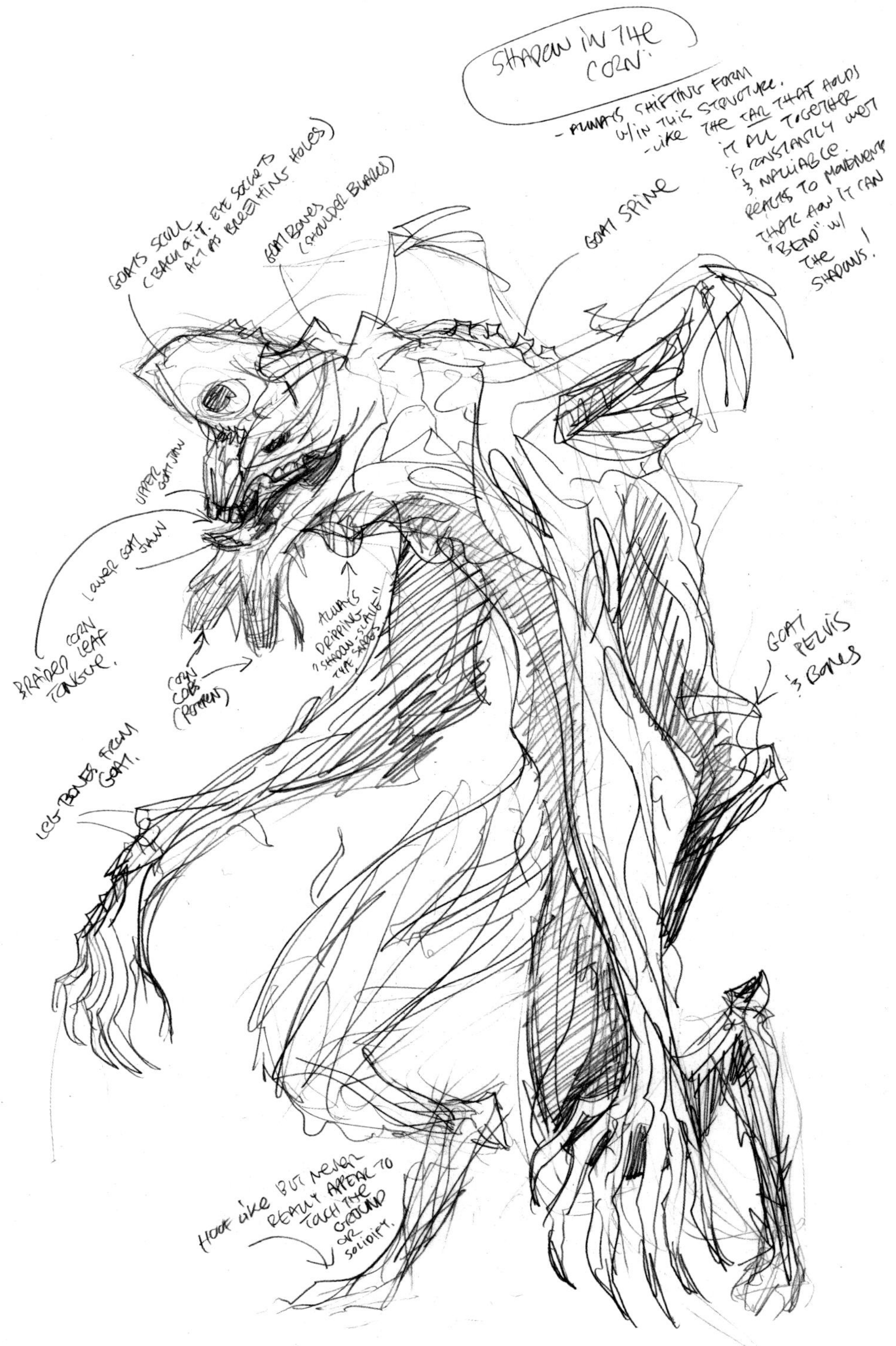

The shadow in the corn creature was challenging. The descriptions of it in the script were super loose, but I clung onto its construction of goats, bones, blood, mud, shadow creatures, souls it absorbed, and corn stalks . . . and I came up with this thing. Researching voodoo and hoodoo talismans and objects, I found that they were amazingly crafted out of ordinary objects and materials and bound together with ordinary things, as well. So it seemed fitting to toss all of those elements onto a page to see what kind of monster I could make. The jaw and the thing on top of its head were made of a goat's skull. Protruding out of its chin were two corn husks. It had the spine and hips from the goat, the arms and legs shared similar goat constructions, and the rest just fell into place along the way.

Sally, Janet, and Claire were a lot of fun to play around with. Our story takes place in Louisiana—Joe is from Texas, and I grew up in Houston and traveled the state and Louisiana a bit growing up—so the lay of the land and people were still familiar. I drew a lot from the culture and memories of the people and places I grew up around.

SALLY

STYLISH SUNGLASSES

TOO PUNK?
?

Jason was one of the easiest characters to play around with. As soon as I read Joe's script I knew exactly what he looked like. The most difficult thing to deal with was the axe in his head and the anatomy of its removal. The placement and act of the axe's removal were very specific, and the description in the script was downright creepy. Once I got the surfer head drawn, the rest was gross fun.

Billy was expendable from the get-go, so what better model to use than myself at that age? He's a bit more handsome than yours truly but served his purpose nonetheless.

I had the most difficult time with Alcebee and the Lawman. Their characters and personalities were so well defined in the script, I knew I couldn't screw them up. The story would fall apart if readers didn't believe those characters on first sight. In the end, I got really attached to these two guys. Sounds silly now, but it was pretty difficult to kill them off in the story. Sappy, I know, but there you go.

I made a final height chart of all the characters for reference. Here's the one I worked out for this book:

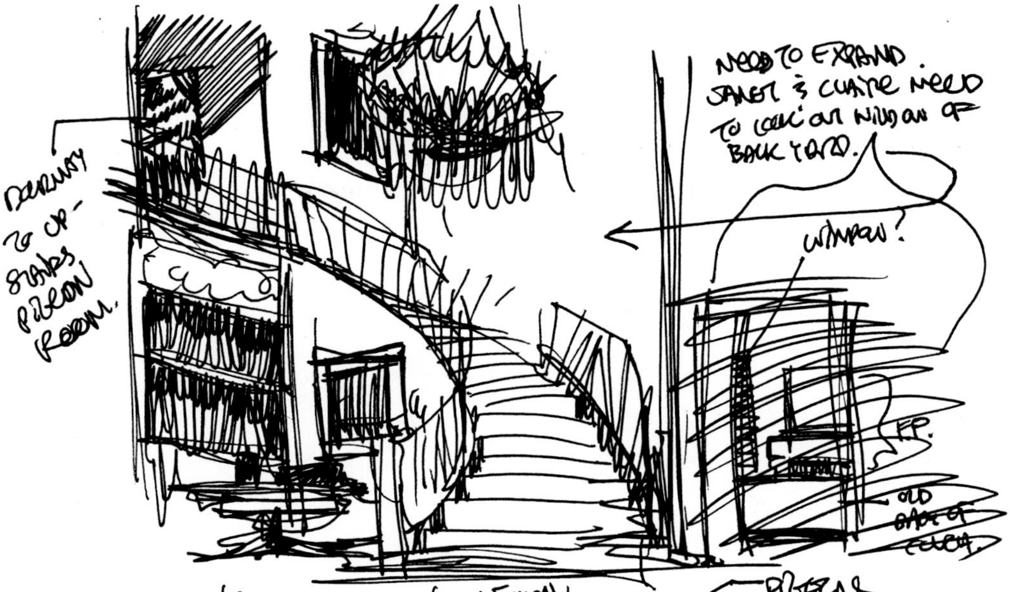

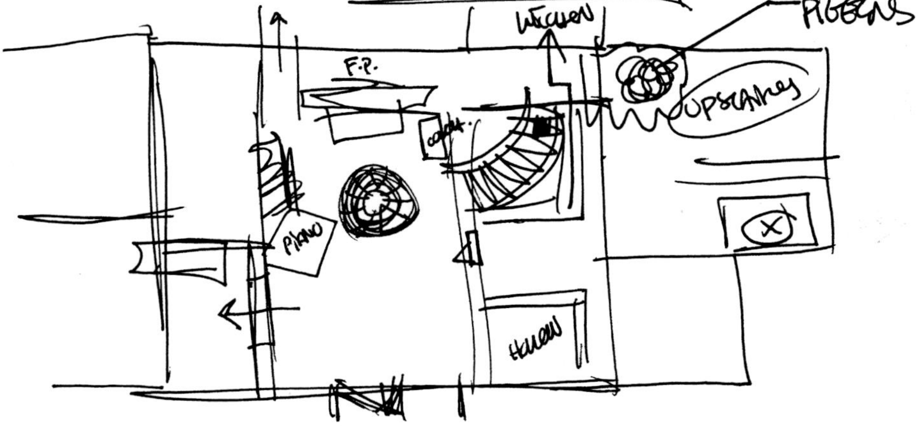

The house was a character in and of itself in the story, and I wanted to bring that out in the final art as well. I pulled a lot of reference from slave plantations, the old, rickety, two-story bay house we used to visit outside of Galveston when I was a kid, and the mansion that was used in the *Thriller* episode of "Pigeons from Hell" that inspired Joe in writing this version. It was an important source for him, so I began the layout with that in mind and expanded from there. Everything had to lead up the stairs and back to the central living room with the fireplace, so hopefully the flow and pitfalls of its designs reflected the mansion from the television show. I would have loved to expand more on its nooks and crannies. The house was, by far, my favorite character in the story.

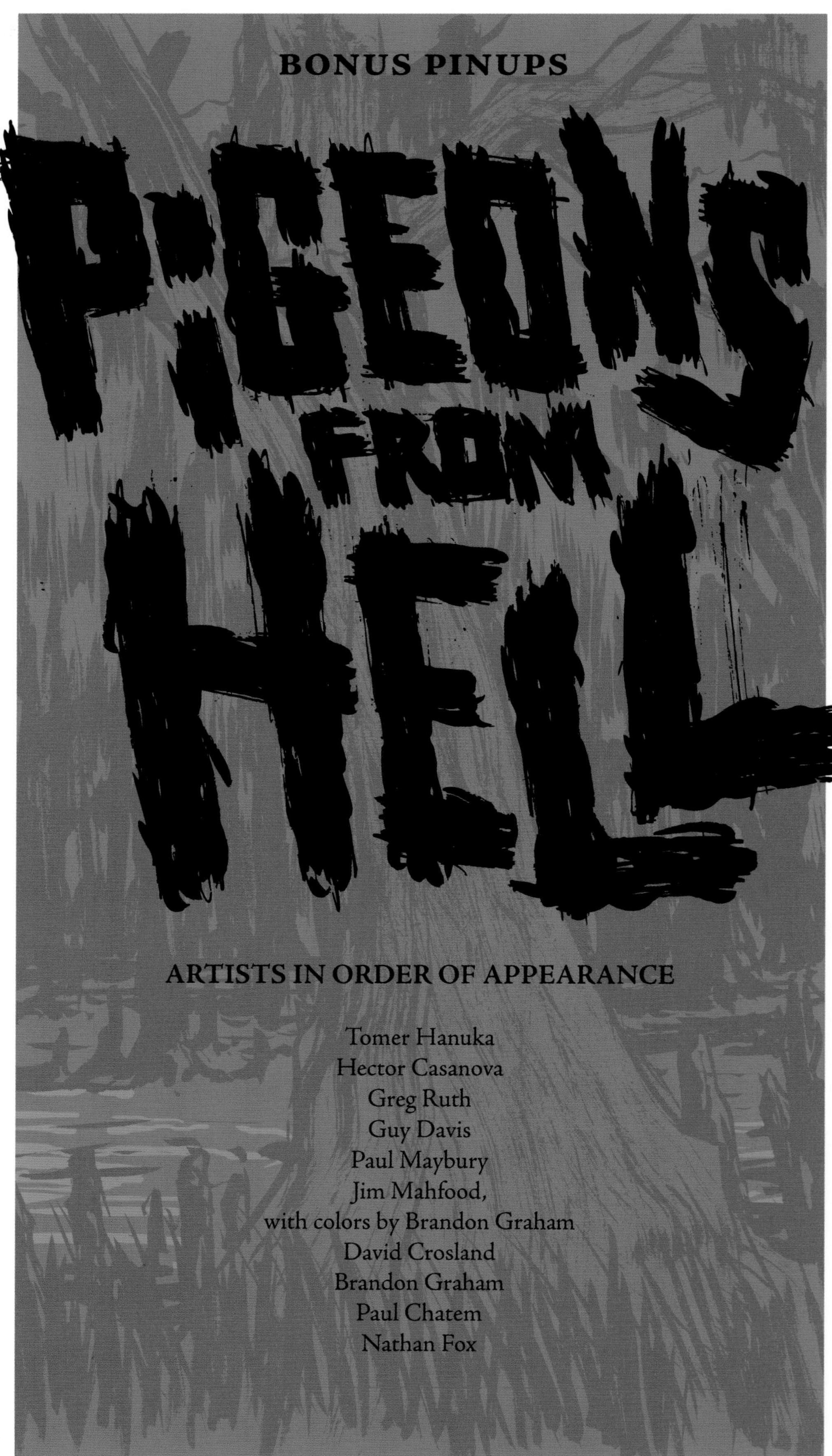
BONUS PINUPS
PIGEONS FROM HELL
ARTISTS IN ORDER OF APPEARANCE
Tomer Hanuka
Hector Casanova
Greg Ruth
Guy Davis
Paul Maybury
Jim Mahfood,
with colors by Brandon Graham
David Crosland
Brandon Graham
Paul Chatem
Nathan Fox

SALLYG

robert 3.
TK'
TAK
crom.
BRANDON FROM SEATTL3.
FROM HELL
ALL FLED, ALL DONE
SO LIFT ME ON THE PYRE:
THE FEAST IS OVER,
THE LAMPS EXPIRE.

P. CHATEM